Whatever Happened
to
English?

Whatever Happened to English?

First Edition

Dean Christensen

Published 2021

ISBN: 9798772085288

Independently Published

Subjects: English language, English grammar, Standard Written English, American English Usage, American English Punctuation

Front cover photo by spaxiax. Used under license from Shutterstock.com

Cover design: GLC

For all who value

clear, coherent, consistent, and correct

Standard Written English.

Contents

According to the National Center for Educational Statistics (NCES), 21 percent of adults in the United States (about 43 million) fall into the illiterate/functionally illiterate category. Nearly two-thirds of fourth graders read below grade level, and the same number graduate from high school still reading below grade level. This puts the United States well behind several other countries in the world, including Japan, all the Scandinavian countries, Canada, the Republic of Korea, and the UK.

– Amy Rea

Nobody who thinks or writes can be above grammar. It is like saying, 'I'm a creative genius, I'm above concepts'—which is the attitude of modern artists. If you are 'above' grammar, you are 'above' concepts; and if you are 'above' concepts, you are 'above' thought. The fact is that then you are not above, but far below, thought. Therefore, make a religion of grammar.

– Ayn Rand

Preface

Plenty of exceptional books on English grammar, writing, usage, punctuation, and vocabulary are readily available today; I've listed several of them in the bibliography. It isn't my intention to add another one to that expansive list. Such an effort would be both pointless and inadequate because, while I enjoy the study of grammar—and I do sometimes call myself a "grammarian"—I am by no means the grammar "expert" that many of those writers are. Besides, I'd probably bore you to death. I sincerely hope I won't do that here.

So what *do* I hope to accomplish? This book is a compilation and revision of many *The Dean's English* blog posts I've written over the past five and a half years; I want to make them as accessible as possible to my millions of adoring fans.[1] In addition, I've included many brand-new essays to enrich your grammar and enhance your life.

As I explain in the Introduction, the title "Whatever Happened to English" is both tongue-in-cheek and serious, which I suppose is like saying it's "funny/not funny." I hope you will find the following pages to be educational or entertaining, regardless of your proficiency with the Mother Tongue.

Hopefully, it will be both.

Dean Christensen
November 2021

---

[1] Okay, "millions" and "adoring" may be stretching it a bit, for which I do apologize.

Introduction

Growing up, I had a mother who cared deeply about writing and speaking English "correctly," even though she was a farmer's daughter with only a Mid-Western small-town high school education. Her passion rubbed off on me.

Although my parents had little worldly wealth and no formal education beyond high school, they valued knowledge and somehow acquired stimulating books for their kids, including the twenty-volume *Golden Book Encyclopedia* set (purchased one volume per week at the local grocery store), several Junior Deluxe Edition classics, and the sixteen-volume set of *Reader's Digest Condensed Classics for Young Readers.* I remember spending long hours reading those books.

In the eighth grade, I was tall, skinny, shy, uncoordinated, bucktoothed, and bespectacled. Yep, a real geek. My self-confidence hovered somewhere between a snake's belly and a lizard's tail. Bored one day, I decided to actually look at the books in my parents' own sparsely stocked bookcase—a three-foot-long two-shelf bookcase that contained maybe twenty-five volumes. Two titles that no well-adjusted junior high kid in the universe could possibly notice caught my eye for some reason: *30 Days to a More Powerful Vocabulary* and *Word Power Made Easy.* I borrowed and devoured them. That year, through those books, seeds were planted for what I eventually became: a logophile,[2] usage snoot, grammarian, and "language maven"—a term intended by linguists like popular author Stephen Pinker to be a good cut, damning with faint praise—which I nonetheless claim and wear proudly.[3] Naively,

---

[2] A logophile (pronounced LOG-a-file) is a person who loves words. From the Greek *logos* (*word*) and *philos* (*love*).
[3] *Maven* is a Yiddish word meaning "one who is experienced or knowledgeable; an expert."

possibly, but proudly. It was the beginning of a new lease on life for this lad's anemic self-image.

Many professional linguists see themselves as The Custodians of the Language, who alone sit in judgment on the mother tongue. They scoff at usage snoots like me, interlopers in their realm who supposedly major in grammatical minors and nitpick endlessly at others' misuse of language. In their view, language mavens cling tenaciously to an outdated notion that English has a "correct" form that must remain unchanged forever. They are certain that grammarians insist on silly and long-ago debunked rules such as "Never end a sentence with a preposition" and "Never split an infinitive"—neither of which has been an issue in grammar manuals or with most grammarians for over a hundred years. Rest assured, that straw man argument does not apply to me and is not what I'm about.

My purpose in these pages isn't to wag a long, bony finger in anyone's face to make them feel bad about their use of language and grammar. Further, I fully realize that English is an ever-evolving language, and I have no intention of preserving the current version in stone tablets.

My purpose—in some ways my *life's mission*—is twofold: (1) to promote Standard Written English (SWE) so that speakers and writers of American English can communicate more effectively, and (2) to do what I can to resist today's cultural slide toward semiliteracy.

Are you ready to join me in that "resistance movement"? Please read on.

Chapter 1
Whatever Happened to English?

First, let's be clear: the title of this book is, more or less, a tongue-in-cheek question.[4] That is to say, on the one hand, nothing has "happened" to English. It is as hale and hearty a language as ever. It is spoken by more people on the planet, with as much richness and diversity as any other spoken or written language.

We native speakers of English are often guilty of taking jabs at our mother tongue—whether good-naturedly or otherwise—because of its many oddities and peculiarities. We sometimes forget that English is the international language of trade and commerce for reasons that go beyond the fact of America's preeminence—and before that, the British Empire's preeminence—on the world stage. English is an expressive, robust, flexible language that is relatively easy for non-native speakers to acquire and use with facility.

In my reading recently, I came across this quote on the exceptional nature of English. Although written seventy years ago, I believe it's still relevant and worth sharing with you:

> *You are fortunate because your language is English. English is a great language; among the world's languages it is perhaps the one that gives the individual the greatest freedom. It is poetic and practical at the same time; it is tremendously rich; it's a sort of all-purpose language. One hundred years ago, the German writer Jakob Grimm wrote of English: "In wealth, good sense, and thrifty order no other of the living languages may be put beside it." He was just one of the many foreigners who envy us*

---

[4] "Tongue-in-cheek": "Characterized by insincerity, irony, or whimsical exaggeration" (Merriam-Webster 2020)

our language; there is almost nothing you can't do with it.[5]

I'm an advocate of learning foreign languages; I've formally studied several of them. If you haven't done so, please do study another language, if for no other reason than to keep your mind nimble or to deepen your appreciation of a different culture. But remember: if you read or speak English, be humbly grateful. It is a great language.

A disclaimer: While this book is a celebration of Standard Written English, I by no means intend to denigrate the spoken or written English of cultures whose style of speaking and writing isn't considered "standard." In one's home and within one's culture, we all can—and should—speak and write in ways that are comfortable and meaningful in those contexts.

You may notice that not every chapter or essay here fits neatly under the category of "grammar." Some items are opinion pieces on language-related topics, whether grammar "pet peeves" or observations on the use and misuse of language in America today (often in social media, emails, and text messages). Some items are topics of interest to me—holiday-themed essays, for example. And I've included a few words near the end on a subject near and dear to my heart: the importance of copyediting and the role of the copyeditor.

---

[5] Rudolf Flesch, *The Art of Readable Writing* (New York: Harper & Brothers Publishers, 1949), 206. In fairness, there are contrary opinions, such as this one by a noted linguist: "The common idea that English dominates the world because it is 'flexible' implies that there have been languages that failed to catch on beyond their tribe because they were mysteriously rigid. I am not aware of any such languages." (John McWhorter, "English Is Not Normal," November 13, 2015, https://aeon.co)

The Effect of Social Media on Written English Today

Speaking of social media, some of you may question my use of examples from Facebook, Twitter, Instagram, or email, arguing that "informal" communications like those don't count, that nobody cares how careful or "correct" those writings are. You are free to disagree—and you may be right in doing so. However, I happen to be of the apparently rapidly disappearing population of English speakers and writers who still care about even those so-called informal writings. I have two rationales for that: (1) We need to write clearly and coherently so that people understand our messages with a minimum of effort—that's just being considerate; and (2) how we write on those platforms—the only place where most of us write these days—reflects on our level of literacy and even (shall I say it?) intelligence. Yes, I know. Many of us who can't write or spell very well are highly intelligent—far more so than I, undoubtedly. But why not let our writing more or less reflect that intelligence?

If you haven't given up on me yet, I invite you to keep reading. My purpose here, and, in many ways, in life, is to promote and celebrate Standard Written English.

As I get older, I am generally less likely to care what others think. At least, that's what I hope is happening. I've always been a pleaser who cares—often too much—what people think. This is not a brag; it's a confession of a weakness. I inherited the tendency from my father, a kind soul who was longsuffering and considerate to a fault.

Language is one of those topics that I feel strongly about. I know the controversies about what constitutes correct grammar, or even if there is a such a thing as "correct" grammar. I am familiar with the scholarly literature on the conflict between the descriptivist and prescriptivist camps. The prescriptivist—in simplistic terms, one who believes there are prescribed language usages and right and wrong grammar and punctuation and ways of writing and speaking—is the language conservative, the traditionalist. The descriptivist—

again in simplistic terms, one who does not believe in such prescriptive approaches to language, who does not tend to label usage differences as "wrong," who believes that the way to approach grammar is the way of the disinterested observer, who merely notes how people use language and that however it is used by that person, or those people is the correct way— is the language liberal or progressive. I prefer to think of myself as a "prescriptive descriptivist" or a "descriptive prescriptivist," depending on my mood. I am somewhere in the middle of the continuum between the two camps.

So I can be opinionated about English usage and grammar. I feel strongly that punctuation serves a useful purpose in making our writing more comprehensible and less ambiguous. I believe that people who either don't know how to use punctuation correctly or don't give a fig about it are likely not to communicate as effectively as they otherwise could. Frankly, I'm turned off by poorly punctuated writing and usage that does not conform to the conventions of Standard Written English—to the extent that I will often quit reading whatever it is. The writer has told me something about him- or herself, and I'm not impressed. I have to know and love that person to want to keep slogging through.

Call me a grammar snob if you must. The brilliant David Foster Wallace coined the term "language snoot" for people like me, and it's not meant as a pejorative. He was a language snoot himself, and that is probably the only thing he and I have in common. "Language maven" is another term, one with a more pejorative connotation. Stephen Pinker and John McWhorter—the former a psychologist (or psycho-linguist) and the latter a linguist, both of whose thinking and writing I enjoy—use that term. They are not well pleased with language snoots, thinking, I suppose, that we are relics of an earlier age—the age of Robert Lowth, for example, whose 1838 classic, *A Short Introduction to English Grammar with Critical Notes*, set the standard for grammar school instruction for generations of English-speakers.

I do not believe that English usage and grammar are set in stone, nor that we should still teach the doctrines of Dr.

8

Lowth. I do not believe that English is unmalleable or unchanging, or that it should be. English is a dynamic language, always changing—sometimes not for the better, but that's my opinion—because it is a living language. It's not a so-called dead language, like Latin, from which so much of our language is derived.

But to get back to my thought about getting older, I don't care as much about what people may think of me now, in my sixties, as I did in my thirties. So you will find me stubbornly opinionated about language from time to time. Let the chips fall where they may. I still have enough of the scourge of "considerateness" flowing through my veins to keep from not caring at all—and I do care about people in general. If you and I could sit down together and have a chat, I would care about you and let you know that I do.

But (and this is a big "but"),[6] my critical mind, my copyeditor's eye, and my descriptive-prescriptivist approach to language will cause me to tell it like it is (at least in my view), and you may not agree with everything I say here. I am fine with that. Perfectly fine. But if I can make you think or care about Standard Written English a little bit more—manifested in clearer, more comprehensible text messages, tweets, emails, social media posts, letters (including cover letters when applying for a job), school essays, master's theses, and book manuscripts—then I will consider my purpose accomplished and this book a success.

If "correction" is forthcoming in these pages, I hope it is done in the spirit of Roman Emperor Marcus Aurelius, who learned from a grammarian named Alexander "not to leap on mistakes, or captiously interrupt when anyone makes an error of vocabulary, syntax, or pronunciation . . ." I have not always been so gracious with my loved ones, but I'm getting better as I approach the golden years. Aurelius went on: ". . . but neatly to introduce the correct form of that particular expression by

---

[6] And yes, I'm aware that I've begun two consecutive paragraphs with a conjunction (*but*), as well as this sentence (*and*). For all my overly old-fashioned grammarians, please see my essay below, "Zapping Three Grammar Myths."

way of answer, confirmation, or discussion of the matter itself rather than its phrasing—or by some other such felicitous prompting."[7] To my (ahem!) credit, I have made it known long ago on my website, in my blog, and on social media that I will never "leap on mistakes" made by others in those places. First, because it is embarrassing to the speaker-writer; second, because, if I'm wrong, I would embarrass myself; third, because friendships in life are hard enough to come by—I certainly don't need to lose the few I have, even if only in cyberworld.

So back to the title question: Whatever Happened to English? Let's begin to answer that with a few words about grammar.

Why Study Grammar?

Bryan Garner wrote, "Perhaps the most important reason for learning about grammar is that language is basic to almost everything we do—and the more nearly you can master it, the more effectively you'll think, speak, and write. . . . A knowledge of grammar is fundamental to critical thinking."[8]

This doesn't mean we have to know how to diagram sentences or write grammatically perfect English at all times. (I know that I don't!) Rather, we aim for a solid grasp of the basics of good usage, syntax, and punctuation—what copyeditors sometimes call the "mechanics" of English—the things that help our language to work better so we communicate more clearly and coherently.

Another word for that is grammar.

---

[7] Marcus Aurelius, *Meditations* 1:10 (UK: Penguin Books, 2006), 5.
[8] Garner, *The Chicago Guide to Grammar, Usage, and Punctuation* 2016, 5.

What *Is* Grammar?

The word *grammar* conjures up uncomfortable memories for many of us as an abstruse subject in school,[9] with its myriad of confusing rules and obtuse sentence diagrams. In classical Greek and Latin, *grammar* (from the Greek *grammatikos*) meant "letters" and referred to the entire range of arts and letters that constituted the scope of learning of the educated person. Much later, in the 17th century, the definition of grammar had become narrowed to *the rules of language.*

"Who makes those 'rules of language?'" you may ask. There is no Department of English in the federal government, no committee of effete grammar snobs whose mission is to establish the "approved," "proper," or "correct" way of writing Standard English. The so-called rules of language evolve over time as people—like you and me—write and speak so that (one hopes) others can understand them. Eventually, those ways of writing become generally accepted in educated society and codified in widely accepted grammar books as The Way of writing, or, to put it succinctly, The Rules of Language. So I supposed I could loosely answer the above question this way: You and I make the rules of language.

I often say that grammar—the rules of language—are to writing what the "rules" in the Department of Motor Vehicle's handbook are to driving. Many of those are more or less arbitrary, but they help us drive more safely so that we get where we want to go. Grammar is like that. We follow the "rules of language" so we can get where we want to go in our written and spoken communications.

Occasionally, people who know what I do as a blog writer and copyeditor will ask me to recommend resources to help with their writing and grammar. One time, a person posted such a request on social media, and when I said I'd be happy to recommend some resources, so please send me your email address so I can send you the list and some helpful links, I

---

[9] *Grammar* school, as it was once known.

never heard from them again. It makes us afraid, writing and grammar does. It's a fearful topic. We run scared.

We have a love–hate relationship with grammar: we love the *idea* of writing—after all, there's that book inside our heads waiting to come out. All we need do is write it down. Or we love that we're working on a college degree, and college, as we discovered, requires a good deal of writing—but it must be *effective* writing (you know, writing that other people can *understand* and not have to jot nasty comments in the margins like, "What the [heck] are you saying here?"). Such writing involves at least a modest grasp of grammar fundamentals. And therein lies the proverbial rub. Writing is like playing the piano—everybody wishes they could do it, but few invest the time and effort needed to actually do it—or do it well, anyway.

And our memories of early experiences with grammar and writing are often negative. We remember the knuckle-rappings and the sittings-in-corners-with-dunce-caps-on[10] because we couldn't diagram a sentence, or because we said, "Me and Johnny want to play ball," or because we confused *your* and *you're*—and we wished Scotty could just beam us up into yonder heavens.

When I was a wee lad of six or seven, my next-door neighbor and playmate was a boy named Leslie, one year younger than I, who mixed up his *heres* and *theres*. He'd motion to me and say, "Come there, Dean, and look at this neat frog." Or "Let's play hide-and-seek. Do you see that tree over here? Go here and count to 100 while I hide." Playing with Leslie was confusing. I was no grammar prodigy, but even then I knew the difference between *here* and *there*. I'm sure Leslie had his knuckles rapped in school—or maybe he *should* have had them rapped.[11]

---

[10] I'm using figurative language here.
[11] A disclaimer for teachers, parents, therapists, social workers, and other potentially horrified readers: I'm kidding about the knuckle-rapping. Of course I'm kidding! I'd much prefer a paddling to a knuckle-rapping.

So people hate grammar as adults. They can still feel the pain in their knuckles thirty years later. Somewhere along the line they decided that nobody was going to make them pay attention to grammar again, and if they want to say, "Ain't nobody gonna learn me no stinkin' grammar," well, they can just *say* it, dad-gummit!

Can we "save" English? It doesn't need saving so much as it needs some Tender Loving Care. The remaining pages are my special blend of TLC. We will begin where most of us live when it comes to the written word: the realm of usage and the many uncertainties that plague our language.

Chapter 2
Usage Uncertainties

Some pairs of similar words are commonly confused in speech and in writing. There is no "speech-checker" to catch our oral miscues, unless we hang out with grammar snobs who don't  care if they maintain friendly terms with us. And with technology as advanced as Microsoft Word's spelling-and-grammar checker is, it doesn't catch everything. How well do you know the differences between the twenty-five or so pairs of words that follow? I've selected them because I run across them so often.

Lay vs. Lie – Let's Sort Out the Confusion

I will begin at the beginning. I have concluded that the *lay–lie* puzzle may be the number one grammar conundrum in the English-speaking world. The confusion is nearly universal. Writers and speakers everywhere get it wrong. All the time.

Popular songs through the years have not helped. I think of Bob Dylan's "Lay, lady, lay, lay across my big brass bed." And Eric Clapton's "Lay down, Sally, and rest you in my arms." Let's not forget Simon and Garfunkel's "The Boxer," which laments of "running scared, laying low, seeking out the poorer quarters where the ragged people go." Unfortunately, the *lays* in all these examples do not follow recognized usage conventions. Now we have an entire generation or two of adults who think that "lay" (or "laid") are the only correct forms of the verb, and that "lie" refers to the words of politicians and media pundits.

So what exactly is the problem? And what's the solution?

First, let's have **some definitions**. The intransitive verb *(vi)*[12] *lie* means to recline or be situated. As an intransitive, *lie* cannot take a direct object. But **lay**, meaning to put down or arrange, is always a transitive verb *(vt)*[13]—it must have a direct object. It is always something you do *to* someone or something—even if that "something" is yourself, as in, "Now I lay me down to sleep." I'll give more examples below, but first, here's a simple chart:

Verb	Present	Past	Present Participle
1. **lay** *(vt)*	lay	laid	laying
2. **lie** *(vi)*	lie	lay	lying

Here are **some examples** of how to correctly use *lay* (#1 above):

- Present: "Honey, please lay the baby (direct object) in the crib for her nap."

- Present: "Let us *lay* our heads (direct object) on our pillows and get some sleep."

- Present participle: "Bob is out back laying bricks for the new barbecue."

- Past: "We *laid* our heads (direct object) on our pillows."

- Past: "She *laid* the baby (direct object) in his crib for his nap."

---

[12] A fuller definition: An intransitive verb "takes a subject but not a direct object because it is capable of making a complete statement without the aid of an object." (Bryan A. Garner, *The Chicago Guide to Grammar, Usage, and Punctuation*, 485.)
[13] A transitive verb takes a direct object (e.g., "We saw **the car**"). (Garner, 487.)

Here's a trick to help you remember: When we mean "put" (or "place"), we use *lay*. Or when we are doing something <u>to</u> something, we use *lay*. We never use *lay* to describe lying down (unless it's past tense—see the chart).

Here are some examples of when to use the intransitive verb *lie* (#2 above):

- Present: "Sheila went to the beach to *lie* on the sand."

- Present: "It's time for me to *lie* down and take my nap."

- Present: "Come here, Spot, and *lie* down. *Lie* down, Spot!"

- Present: "The bandit decided to *lie* low (not *lay* low) until the heat was off."

- Present participle: "Spot is *lying* on her bed while we eat dinner."

- Present participle: "The children are *lying* on their mats for their afternoon nap."

- Past: "When Sheila went to the beach last weekend, she *lay* on the sand all day." (Note, the past tense of *lie* is **not** *laid*. You use laid only when talking about putting something somewhere —"The Ladies Guild *laid* out a feast for all the party-goers to enjoy.")

- Past: "I *lay* (not *laid*) in bed for two hours during my nap."

- Past: "Spot is such a good dog. She *lay* (not *laid*) on her bed all through dinner."

- Past: "The bandit *lay* low (not *laid* low) for two years and then came out of hiding."

16

I hope this has been helpful. Now it's time for me to *lay* my books down on the shelf and go *lie* down for my afternoon nap.

It's vs. Its – Which Should It Be?

Next to the *lay–lie* confusion, this question may be the most vexing for writers of English. But it need not be if we keep in mind that one of the principal uses of an apostrophe is to fuse two words into one—that is, to make a contraction. In this case, the apostrophe in *it's* always and only makes a contraction of *it is* (or much less frequently, *it has*).

I repeat, *it's* has essentially one meaning in English: *it is*.

Examples:

- "It's (*it is*) a big car." It's (*it has*) got a roomy interior." [*It's got* should be avoided in formal writing.]

- "It's (*it is*) the first day of the rest of your life."

- "It's (*it is*) about time I learned the difference between it's and its."

Which brings me to *its*. *Its* is an adjective, the possessive form of the pronoun *it*—which corresponds to the possessive form of the pronouns *he* (*his*) and *her* (*hers*). Notice there is no apostrophe in *his* or *hers*, and there is no apostrophe in *its*.

Examples:

- "Look at the way the happy dog wags its tail!"

- "Virtue is its own reward."

- "Don't judge a book by its cover."

- "He has made everything beautiful in its time" (Ecclesiastes 3:11, NIV).

Because we know that adding an apostrophe to a noun often makes it possessive, it's easy to understand why we're tempted to make the possessive of *it it's*. But unless we are referring to Stephen King's book and the movie *It* (*It's* genre is horror), or to Cousin It on the Addams Family ("Those are It's comb and sunglasses"), the only time we add the apostrophe is to make the contraction *it is* (or *it has*).

Sank vs. Sunk – Another Common Confusion

The simple past tense of *sink* is *sank*: "Bird sank the 30-foot jump shot at the buzzer." The past participle is *sunk*: "The Dow Jones Industrials *has sunk* to a new low." "Bird had sunk the 30-foot jump shot last week, but tonight he missed it by inches."

However, like *shrank* vs. *shrunk, sank* vs. *sunk* is often confused, even by professional writers. For example: "It was the second hole-in-one in as many days for Rahm during practice play for The Masters. On Monday, he sunk [instead, read that *he sank*] the par-3 4th hole playing next to Fowler and Brendon Todd."[14]

Speaking of *shrank* vs. *shrunk*: Shrank is the commonly accepted past tense and shrunk is the perfect and past perfect of shrink. Let's not forget the infamous movie title *Honey, I Shrunk* [read *Shrank*] *the Kids!*

Quash vs. Squash

Squash – to flatten or soften something by forceful crushing or squeezing, as in squashing a cockroach.

---

[14] Daniel Canova, Fox News online. Retrieved 11/10/20 from https://www.foxnews.com/sports/jon-rahm-skips-golf-ball-over-water-nails-impressive-hole-in-one-ahead-of-masters

Quash – to put down or suppress, as, for example, a rebellion or a rumor.

Be careful not to confuse the two—as most people do, including professional writers and journalists. When someone writes, "They squashed the unfounded rumor," in my mind I'm seeing that cockroach. Yuck. It should be, "They *quashed* the unfounded rumor."

Everyday vs. Every Day

It's easy to forget that "everyday" (one word) is a compound adjective that means "ordinary," "typical," "usual," or "garden variety," as in "Let me slip on my everyday shoes."

"Every day" (two words), on the other hand, is an adverb that means, well, "every day," as in, "His wife visits him at the lake every day," or, "We walk the dog every day."

Here's the heading of an ad from the website of a national company I saw recently: "Tacos everyday." Nope. I don't think they mean everyday (as in run-of-the-mill) tacos; they mean tacos you can eat every day. The difference may be slight but definite. After all, if "everyday" is correct, why not "everyweek" or "everymonth" or "everyyear"?

The vast majority of the time, we mean "every day," but every day I see it written incorrectly; it has become an everyday thing on social media and wall plaques.

Your vs. You're

Remember, when you mean **you are,** as in
- "You are so funny"
- "You are sixteen, going on seventeen,"
you may substitute the contraction *you're*, as in
- "You're so funny."
- "You're sixteen, going on seventeen."

Employ that apostrophe!

When you mean "belonging to you," you may substitute the possessive pronoun **your**, as in

- "Your jokes are so funny."
- "Your seventeenth birthday is coming up soon."

To review:

- You are = you're

- Belonging to you = your

It's not difficult.

A lot vs. Alot

A lot is two words. And *always* two.

- "I love you *a lot*, little brother!"
- "This is *a lot* of information to digest."
- "I see *a lot* misspelled as *alot* a lot."

Please remember: *a lot* is always *two* words."[15]

To vs. Too

These two are frequently confused.

Waiting at a red light on my way to work one day, I read this misspelled message stenciled in white Gothic letters across the rear window of the car in front of me: "To [read *Too*] Blessed to Be Stressed." On either side of it were silhouettes of Mickey Mouse heads. (I kid you not.)

To most often (but not exclusively) functions as a preposition.

- "She went to the store."
- "We went down to the sea in ships."

---

[15] And yet, *allot* is one word—with a hugely different meaning: "to assign as a share or a portion. "Grandpa decided to allot one-fifth of his estate to each of his five grandchildren."

Too frequently means *also* or *so*.

- "You can come to the party too."
- "You did too snore in your sleep."

Too often serves as an adverbial intensifier meaning something like *very, excessively, extremely,* or *quite*. It's often used with adjectives like *much, many, difficult, hard, soft, fast, slow, funny, runny, bright,* or *sad*.

- "Your baby is too cute!" (NOT "to cute.")
- "English grammar is too hard." (NOT "to hard.")

Every time someone types "to funny," I immediately picture them, fist in the air, going on a quest to find funny.

your ⓔcards
someecards.com

Home in vs. Hone in

To "*hone*" (not hone *in*) is to sharpen or develop something:

- "The woman *honed* her writing skills by writing 250 words a day."

To "home in" on something is to make it a point of focus, like going home:

- "The candidate *homed in* on the issue of taxes in his campaign speech."

Hone in as an expression is never correct. It's *home in*.

Here are more incorrect examples I've seen:

An online news headline: "Election 1 day away: [Candidate 1] to blitz 4 key states as [Candidate 2] hones in [read *homes in*] on Pennsylvania." The subtitle repeats the error: "Candidate 2, Candidate 1 hone in [read *home in*] on key battleground states on eve of Election Day."

"With so many stats swirling around, it can be difficult to know which stats to hone in [read *home in*] on." –MLB.com

"Keep your eyes open and your ears *honed into* [read *homed into*—or better, *attuned to*] this page. I will announce the time and date of the celebration soon." – from a website

Taken Aback vs. Taken Back

When you're shocked or stunned, you're *taken aback*. You're *taken back* in time or memory.

"The man was taken aback when told he resembled Moe of the Three Stooges."

You may be taken *back* to your childhood when you catch the whiff of a brand-new comic book or hear a familiar hymn playing on the radio, or taken back to a former girlfriend or boyfriend when you smell the same cologne he or she wore.

Used to vs. Use to

Used to is the correct form. It is past tense, so we add the -*d*. I understand that the *d* and *t* are blended together when we say it, but remember to add the *d* when spelling it. Always. I repeat: always.

- "Bill *used to* go to all his alma mater's football games."
- "I *used to* be good at math."

Based on vs. Based off of

A survey I received via email from a restaurant recently started this way: "Based off of your most recent visit to our restaurant, how would you rate the service you received?"

Ouch! I won't keep you in suspense. It's **based on** (or *upon*) something, not based *off of* something, no matter how prevalent the misusage is. Standard English is *based on*.

Set Up vs. Setup

Set up refers to an action; *setup* is a noun.

- The Joneses arrived to *set up* (verb) the food and games.
- During the party, one guest commented, "What a nice *setup* (noun) you have here!"

Log In vs. Login

The same can be said for *log in* vs. *login*: log in is the action, the verb, while login is the noun or adjective.

- "You can *log in* to your online account using the *login* button on the top right corner of the home page.

There vs. Their vs. They're – A (Way Too) Frequent Confusion

There often refers to place or position, or is used as a function word to begin a sentence, or is used for emphasis, as follows:

- "Go stand over there."
- "There are over 42,000 words in this book."
- "That man over there can help you find your hotel room."

Please don't confuse *there* with the possessive personal pronoun *their*. When you're talking about people, use their, not *there*.

- "Their understanding of grammar was mediocre at best."

And please don't confuse either *there* or *their* with *they're*. The apostrophe in *they're* indicates it's a **contraction** of two words: *they are*.

- "My friends are leaving on a jet plane tomorrow. They're returning to their home in Singapore."

There, there. Does that help now?

Bid vs. Bade

The Problem

Here is an example of a situation where my spell-checker cannot catch a common usage error. I found this example in an online news article:

"Digital discount broker E*Trade Financial Corp on Thursday bid farewell [read *bade farewell*] to the precocious baby who starred in the television commercials advertising its trading platform for the last seven years."

The Explanation

There are two common meanings of the verb *bid*: (1) to give expression to (as in the above context): to give expression to one's farewell toward someone or something, and (2) to offer a price, as in bidding on an auction item, a business project, or the purchase of a home.

In the first meaning, the past tense is *bade*: "The staff bade (pronounced either *bad* or *bād*, you choose) farewell to their colleague at her retirement party."

In the second meaning, the past tense is the same as the present tense, *bid*: "I didn't win the antique clock at yesterday's auction because I bid too low."

Keep the two different means of bid in mind and remember: each has its own past tense—*bade* for the first and *bid* for the second.

Bad vs. Badly

Now, let's tackle the *bad* vs. *badly* mix-up. These two are most often misused in the context of how a person feels about something. "I heard that Charles's wife left him when he spent their entire savings on a baseball card, and I feel [*bad* or *badly*—which is it?] for them." The correct answer is *bad*. Yes, it is! (I'm sorry. I feel bad if you got it wrong.)

According to the AP Stylebook, *bad*, used in this way, is an adjective and is the idiomatic equivalent of "I am in bad health" or "I am in a bad emotional state." We correctly use *badly* as an adverb (an adverb modifies verbs, adjectives, or other adverbs). For example, "This author reasons badly, writes badly, and even spells his name badly." That's all grammatically correct, but it makes the author feel bad.

Gist vs. Just

As a kid, my teachers persistently corrected students who sloppily said things like, "I jist tapped that boy a little on his cheek—not enough to knock out that bloody tooth there on the floor." So when we grew up, some of us were so paranoid about not saying "jist" when we should have said "just" that we now reflexively say "just" when we should say "gist" (pronounced jist). Grammarians call this a hypercorrection.

Confused yet? No? Let me keep trying. *Gist* means "the main point or part." When we're talking about the main point or part of this book with all our friends (yes, *all* of them), it's okay to call it the *gist* of the book. Just don't call it the *just*.

Moot vs. Mute

Then there is the infamous *moot–mute* mix-up. *Moot*, according to the dictionary, means "deprived of practical significance; made abstract or purely academic." A "moot point," is one that is essentially irrelevant or unimportant to the topic at hand, or impossible to discuss intelligently for whatever reason. *Mute*, on the other hand, is the button we press on the remote when the commercial comes on. To mute (verb) something is "to muffle, reduce, or eliminate the sound of" that thing.

When used as a noun, a *mute* is "a device attached to or inserted into a musical instrument to soften or alter its tone," or is a person who cannot or does not talk.

By now, this is a moot point, but the word we want to use when talking about, well, a moot point is *moot*. (It rhymes with boot, or toot.)

Disinterested vs. Uninterested

Ninety-nine in one hundred people will say they are uninterested in grammar, punctuation, syntax, word usage, and all that good stuff. That means they couldn't care less. Those ninety-nine are not reading this book, but you are of the One Percent, and I congratulate you. Many of those ninety-nine people would say they are *disinterested* in grammar, but, alas, if they were disinterested, it would simply mean they were unbiased or impartial. A "disinterested party" is a person or group who doesn't stand to make or lose anything in a situation.

Members of a jury pool should be *disinterested* concerning the court case to be tried—not that they have no interest in it (which is a moot point whether they do or not), but that they have no strong feelings one way or the other about whether the defendant is guilty or innocent. They are disinterested members of the community.

The uninterested ones are those other ninety-nine who aren't reading this. Thank *you* for your interest.

Insure vs. Ensure

Which is appropriate? People often use *insure* when it should be *ensure*.

Insure – restricted entirely to financial contexts (think *insurance*).

Ensure – in almost all other contexts, such as, "I want to ensure that you understand the difference between *insure* and *ensure*."

Advise vs. Advice

To *advise* (an action) is a verb and *advice* (a thing) is a noun that refers to the information given or received in the act of advising.

- "Many people have given me sound *advice* about a lot of things in my lifetime, some of which I have heeded. Let me *advise* you to heed wise, godly *advice* when you receive it."

Confusing these two words is understandable because of another pair of words, *vise* and *vice*, which are homonyms: they are pronounced exactly the same (vīs). A vise is a tool attached to a workbench that is used to hold something securely in place. A vice, as people generally use it, is a "habitual and usually trivial defect or shortcoming."

Advise and *advice* are not homonyms. They are pronounced differently and mean different things.

27

"Between X *to* X" vs. "Between X *and* X"

The second usage is preferred in Standard English. I wouldn't say "our new cars cost between $20,000 **to** $25,000" but rather "our new cars cost between $20,000 **and** $25,000." Between fifty **and** sixty percent of writers and speakers of English confuse these expressions.

If you don't use *between* and instead use *from* or *in*, you can safely use *to*. For example, "From fifteen **to** twenty thousand people moved out of California last month. In four **to** six weeks, they will be happily settled in their new cities."

Memento vs. Momento

When I stopped into a gift shop to purchase a souvenir, the clerk said it would make a "nice momento." This is a common spoken mistake; the correct word is *memento*.

Momento is **not** a word. At least not in English.

It's understandable why a lot of people (and I do mean a *lot* of people) get this one wrong. I can think of two reasons: (1) *Momento* is a Spanish word that means *moment*, and (2) it makes sense that the souvenir from your vacation will help you remember a particular moment—thus a *momento*, right? Sorry, but no. Again, sadly, *momento* is not a word in English.

Here's how to keep it straight: a *memento* is a MEMory aid that helps you reMEMber a person, place, or thing, or comMEMorate something. That should be easy to MEMorize.

Sarcasm vs. Irony

The confusion of these two words is particularly bothersome because it is so widespread and the meanings are, well, so different. I frequently hear someone say that so-and-so was being *sarcastic* when they should have used the word *ironic*. Sarcasm is a type of irony, yes, but the two words are not interchangeable. Here's how one dictionary defines *irony*:

"the use of words to express something other than and especially the opposite of the literal meaning." The adjective *ironic* "implies an attempt to be amusing or provocative by saying usually the opposite of what is meant." So, when I step outside on a 106-degree Central Valley summer day and say, "Brrr, it's chilly. Someone get me my jacket!" I'm either (a) insane, (b) sick, (c) using irony, or (d) using sarcasm. (The answer is *c*. . . . but maybe it's *a*.)

Sarcasm, on the other hand, is related to irony, but its emphasis is strongly negative—it is irony's wicked stepsister. Here's the definition of *sarcasm* (which comes from the Greek word meaning "to tear flesh," subtly hinting of its negative meaning): "a sharp and often satirical or ironic utterance designed to cut or give pain." The adjective form, *sarcastic*, "implies an intentional inflicting of pain by deriding, taunting, or ridiculing." I've heard a number of people, usually younger people, describe themselves approvingly as being sarcastic or having a sarcastic brand of humor. It may be true, but I think in most cases the word they should have used was *ironic*. Sarcasm *can* be funny, in the right context and around understanding people, but it's generally not something to aspire to—unless you can make a killing with it as a comedy writer or cartoonist.

Regardless vs. Irregardless

The correct word is *regardless*; *irregardless* is not a word. Well, strictly speaking, it *is* a word according to *Merriam-Webster's Collegiate Dictionary*—a probable blending of *irrespective* and *regardless*—but it's not considered standard usage. *Regardless* already means "without regard," so *irregardless* would have to mean "*not* without regard," a peculiar double negative. The word to use 100 of 100 times is *regardless*, not *irregardless*. It's easier to say and one syllable shorter. Make life easier for yourself and others: use *regardless*; ditch *irregardless*.

Parentheses vs. Parenthesee

(A bonus commonly confused word pair.)

This is kind of a joke, but I have actually heard *parenthesee* used by more than one person. However, *parentheses* is the plural of the singular *parenthesis*, referring to the curved symbol we place around a parenthetical word or phrase. We almost always use those symbols in pairs; thus the plural *parentheses* is more common. (E.g., "Remember to enclose verbal asides in *parentheses* in your script.")

Parenthesee, as the singular form to refer to just *one* of those curved things, is incorrect; it's not a word. Nope, nope, nope. The word is *parenthesis*. (Yes, really!)

Chapter 3
Punctuation Perplexities

*"Punctuation isn't some subtle, arcane concept that's
hard to manage and that probably won't make much
of a difference one way or another. It's not subtle, it's
not difficult, and it can make all the difference in the
world." – Patricia T. O'Conner*

The Lowly Comma: Eight Ways to Fix Its Misuse and Abuse

What punctuation mark has caused more problems than the comma? The comma may be the most abused, misused, overused, and misunderstood punctuation mark of them all.

Author Amy Einshon says that commas are the "copyeditor's nemesis"[16] because comma misuse is one of the toughest grammar nuts to crack. Yes, commas can be difficult, but with a little effort and patience, we can master them (or die trying).[17]

The comma is a delicate punctuation mark—some would say even dainty. It doesn't bear the heavy burden of ending sentences (use the period for that), of marking astonishment (employ the exclamation point!), of asking (roll in the question mark), or of pausing between independent clauses without using a conjunction (hand that one to the semicolon). Its duty is lighter but no less important. To put it simply, the comma indicates a slight pause. But not

---

[16] Einsohn 2011, 95.
[17] Please *don't* die trying.

every place we naturally pause in written communication requires a comma. And sometimes where we don't pause, there a comma must go. How can we solve this confusion?

Rules of grammar seem so restricting, so schoolmarmish. But they do help us make sense of written communication, so let's consider eight basic comma rules. If we master these eight rules, we are well on the road to mastering our very grammatical souls. Aren't you glad you're reading this?

1. Use commas to separate three or more items in a series.

If Strunk and White felt it was important enough to make this the second of eleven "elementary rules of usage" in their classic work, *The Elements of Style*, I can make it the first of my comma rules. Here's an example:

- "Georgie Porgie Puddinpie celebrated National Punctuation Day with his dear wife and four children: Georgie Jr., Porgie Ann, Peter, and Polly."

Notice how I separated each name in the list with a comma, including one before the final name, Polly. That final comma always comes before the conjunction—in this case, *and*. It's called a **series** (or serial) comma, or, if you really want to sound highbrow, an **Oxford** comma.

"**Learn how to cut, marinate, and cook friends!**"

Commas matter.

2. Use a comma to separate independent clauses (i.e., clauses that can stand on their own as complete sentences) **that are joined by a coordinating conjunction.**

The most common coordinating conjunctions make up the acrostic FANBOYS: *for, and, nor, but, or, yet, so)*. Before you go running for a Greek lexicon because this all sounds like, well, Greek, let me illustrate with a biblical quotation. In a recent sermon, a pastor read from Luke 1 about the angel Gabriel's visit to Mary announcing the birth of Jesus. "You will be with child and give birth to a son, and you are to give him the name Jesus" (Luke 1:31 NIV). Do you see the two independent clauses? The first, "You will be with child and give birth to a son," could stand as a sentence by itself. The second, "you are to give him the name Jesus," could also stand alone as a sentence. What joins them is a comma, followed by one of the FANBOYS conjunctions—*and.*

3. Use a comma to set off introductory elements and direct address.

The word "introductory" is a clue: it refers to a word or short phrase at the beginning of a sentence, before the subject and verb—that is, before a clause that can stand alone as a complete sentence. "When I study grammar, my blood boils." "When I study grammar" is the introductory phrase—it can't stand alone as a complete sentence. It is a dependent clause—that is, it is dependent on something else to complete the thought so the reader isn't left hanging, which would not be good. "My blood" is the subject and "boils" is the verb, and taken together the three words can stand alone as a complete sentence. It finishes the thought begun by "When I study grammar."

Sometimes, an introductory element is just one word and is set off from the rest of the sentence by a comma (like *sometimes* at the beginning of this sentence). Not all grammar authorities agree that a comma placed after a single introductory word is necessary if the meaning is clear without it. Use your own judgment, but be consistent.

We also use a comma in direct address: "Dean, it's time to move on." Conversely, if we flip that around, we still need the comma: "It's time to move on, Dean." While we're on the topic of direct address, let's join the growing national movement to restore the missing comma in our greetings, thank-yous, and well wishes. Note the comma placement in these examples: "Happy birthday, Harpo!" "Congratulations, Zeppo!" Thank you, Gummo!" "Howdy-doody, Bozo!" I know that cell-phone texting habits have all but killed that comma, but we must resist and stand firm! Let us make our world a better place for our grandchildren.

4. Use a comma to set off interrupters and appositives.

Interrupters are words or phrases that interrupt the thought of a sentence but are not essential to the meaning of the sentence. You surround the interrupter with commas—one before and one after. You can use parentheses or dashes to do the same thing, if you so choose, but here we're talking about commas. Okay, stop and look at the previous sentence. See the interrupter? The phrase "if you so choose" is not essential to the meaning of the sentence. Mentally take it out and reread the sentence. That's the test of whether you will need to set off a phrase with a pair of commas.

Similarly, when you follow a noun with a word or phrase in order to describe or give more information about it— something called an *appositive*—you need commas: "*Duck Soup*, the Marx Brothers 1933 classic, is on the American Film Institute's list of top 100 all-time films. The phrase "the Marx Brothers 1933 classic" is additional information about the previous noun, *Duck Soup*, and needs to be set off with commas. It's an appositive phrase.

An appositive can go at the end of a sentence as well: "One of AFI's all-time top 100 films is *Duck Soup*, the Marx Brothers 1933 classic." Note the comma after *Soup*. It indicates that what follows is an appositive phrase. The additional information is nice to have and maybe even important, but it's not essential to understanding the sentence. If a word or phrase is essential to the meaning, don't set it off with commas. "One of AFI's top 100 films is the Marx Brothers classic *Duck Soup*." If that's how you choose to write it, then every word is essential to its proper understanding. No commas are needed.

5. Use a comma to separate a direct quotation from its attribution (i.e., who said it).

Here's an example: "'That's pretty straightforward,' said Polly Puddinpie." Notice the comma? We can also flip it around like this: "Polly Puddinpie said, 'That's pretty straightforward.'" Here's one catch: if it's an *indirect* quotation, no quotation marks or comma are required. "Polly Puddinpie said that it was a very simple." See? No quotation marks and no commas. Piece of cake! Here's a tip for students writing papers so you don't get nailed for plagiarism: If you make a direct, word-for-word quotation (as in the first example), give the source appropriate credit. That's called a citation. If you make an indirect quotation, as in the second example, you will still need to give a source citation, even though you changed the words a little. Why's that? Them's just the rules.[18]

6. Use a comma to separate two or more coordinate adjectives describing the same noun.

Now I *know* you're ready to run for the hills. But wait! It's not so bad with an example or two. "For my birthday I want a tall, round, calorie-free, chocolate cake." The noun here (*chocolate cake*) is described with various adjectives.

A simple test will help you decide if and where you need to place commas: the "*and*" test. If you can replace the commas with the word *and*, and it makes sense, the commas are good. Let's try it: "For my birthday I want a round and tall and calorie-free chocolate cake." Yep, that makes sense. Another test is to mix up the order of the adjectives: "For my birthday

---

[18] Yes, I know that's not proper grammar. It should have been "those are the rules."

I want a calorie-free, tall, round chocolate cake." Yep! Still good.[19] Let us eat cake!

7. Use commas to set off dates, place names, titles, and addresses.

- **Dates, when used in a sentence**: "On July 4, 1776, Polly Puddinpie walked her dog downtown." See the comma after *1776*? Strangely, that's how it's done.

- **Place names:** "Polly Puddinpie lived in Philadelphia, Pennsylvania, during the American Revolution. Notice the comma after the state name? Yes, it's supposed to be there.

- **Titles:** "Dr. Polly Puddinpie, M.D., was inspired to open her own medical practice after watching *Dr. Quinn, Medicine Woman* on television. *M.D.* is set off with commas. (And here's a freebie: *Medicine Woman* is an appositive describing *Dr. Quinn*, so there must be a comma after *Quinn*.)

- **Addresses:** Dr. Puddinpie lived at 7 Main Street, Philadelphia, Pennsylvania. Simple, right?

8. Use commas to indicate interdependent clauses and antithetical elements.

- **Interdependent elements.** Okay, don't throw up your hands—this isn't as difficult as it seems. Here are examples of interdependent elements: "The longer the article, the sleepier I get." "The bigger they are, the harder they fall." If it's a short sentence, no comma is needed: "The fewer the better."

- **Antithetical (or contrasting) elements** are set off with a pair of commas: "It's the quality, not the quantity, that counts." "We're at the end, not the beginning, of this long essay."

---

[19] Technically, it is still good. However, it does violate the "rule" of adjective ordering. See that essay elsewhere in this book.

A caveat: the trend in American writing is fewer, not more, commas. Use them judiciously, but follow these guidelines. Doing so will help make your writing more clear, coherent, consistent, and yes, correct.

More On Using Commas in Direct Address

The cartoon here humorously illustrates the importance of

properly punctuating a sentence that involves direct address—that is, when **writing directly to** someone. The standard English convention is to **place a comma after the introductory word or phrase.**

Need some **examples,** friend? Here you go, gentle reader. (Um, notice the two examples there?)

- "Hello, John!"

- "Thanks, Maria."

- "How are you, Pete?"

- "Way to go, Andrea!"

- "You're confusing me, Dean."

Don't leave out those poor, underemployed commas. Let them serve their intended purpose.

And let's not forget these:

- "Happy birthday, Tori!"

- "Merry Christmas, Lou!"

- "¡Feliz Navidad, Luis!"

- "Happy anniversary, Mom and Dad!"

It's almost time for lunch. Let's eat, Grandma!

Five Common Punctuation Errors to Avoid

June Casagrande begins her excellent book on punctuation— one I highly recommend— with this statement: "Punctuation is easy, except when it's not."[20]

Punctuation issues – It's astounding to me how many people write with no punctuation at all—not only in text messages and social media posts and comments, but also in supposedly formal emails[21] and even school/college papers. Their sentences seem to be long, rambling streams of consciousness, sans commas, sans periods, sans capitalization, sans everything.[22] I studied koine Greek in my undergraduate and graduate school days, where we students learned that the New Testament autographs (i.e., the original manuscripts) were written much like this, without punctuation and even without spaces between words. Applying rules of punctuation to text may reflect a buttoned-down, straightlaced mentality—and those rules are essentially arbitrary—but they exist for a reason: readability and understandability.

Whether you're an employee writing a business letter, report, or memo; a job seeker crafting a cover letter to submit with an application; a student working on a dreaded writing assignment for class; or a social-media poster who doesn't want to sound like Doofus McGoofus, you'll want to avoid these common punctuation errors.

1. Quotation marks inside of punctuation. Ninety-nine percent of quotation marks in American English go *outside* of

---

[20] Casagrande 2014, 1.

[21] For example, here's the verbatim text of an email I received from a college student yesterday (the name has been changed): *"Hello thank you for emailing me I'm trying to take psychology 2 with L Robert Springer however it says times to be announced and also said it is a repeat and that it doesn't meet the grade requirements and I need to know a time because I work and i need the latest class possible I'm also trying to take yoga for a pe coarse and that class is also saying time to be announced."*

[22] Okay, maybe not sans *everything*. This is an oblique reference to Shakespeare's "seven ages of man" in *As You Like It*.

adjacent punctuation[23]—specifically, commas, periods, question marks, and exclamation points. For example,

"It's time to take the quiz," said the teacher, "so please close and put away your books." The quotation marks after *quiz* and *books* are outside the comma and the period.

"Have you put away your books yet?" asked the teacher. "Yes, we have!" exclaimed the students. Here the quotation marks properly go outside the question mark and the exclamation point.

There are exceptions, however (aren't there always?). When a question is asked about a quoted statement, the question mark goes outside the quotation mark. "Did I hear the teacher say, 'It's time to take the quiz'"? See the question mark? The questioner is asking about something the teacher said—which was a statement, not a question—so the question mark here goes outside the quotation marks. "Duh! The teacher said, 'It's time to take the test'"! The responder is answering in an exclamatory manner while quoting the teacher's exact words, hence the exclamation point after the quotation marks.

As a general rule, it's safe to say that quotation marks never go inside of periods and commas in American English. Or to state it positively—periods and commas always go inside of quotation marks. There are exceptions, but remember the general rule.

2. Semicolons used instead of colons. A semicolon is used primarily for joining two related independent clauses together without using a period, or a comma with a conjunction. Remember, an independent clause is a group of words that contains a subject and a verb and expresses a complete thought. You can see an example of the proper use of a semicolon in the next section on comma splices, so I won't elaborate further. But the important thing to keep in mind is not to use a semicolon where a colon should be used—a

---

[23] This 99% statistic is made up—but it's probably close to the truth. It may even be a bit low in American English. British English is quite a different bloody matter, bloke, and is a topic for another day.

common mistake. A colon is used mainly to tell your reader that something follows, and it should be placed after a complete sentence (or independent clause). For example:

- "All job applicants who are invited for an interview must remember two important things: dress appropriately and show up on time."

All that precedes the colon is a complete sentence. "All job applicants . . . must remember two important things." But that leaves the reader hanging, waiting for more, and asking silently, "What 'important things' do I need to remember?" The colon tells her the suspense is only momentary: to "dress appropriately and show up on time." Don't confuse the semicolon with the colon since they have quite distinct functions.

Oh, another common use for the semicolon is to promote tidiness in long, complex lists: "Growing up, I lived in London, England; London, Ontario, Canada; and London, Kentucky." (See below for more on the semicolon.)

3. Comma splices. A comma splice occurs when a comma— dainty critter that it is—is called on to perform heavy-duty punctuation beyond its pay grade: ending complete sentences. Here's an example of the incorrect use of commas:

- "I graduated with honors from the university last year, it was tempting to go straight into a master's program, I wanted to get real-world job experience first."

There are two comma splices joining together three independent clauses. The writer should have used periods in place of the commas, OR a period and a semicolon, OR a period and a comma + conjunction. Here's what those three options look like:

- "I graduated with honors from the university last year. It was tempting to go straight into a master's program. I wanted to get real-world job experience first."

- "I graduated with honors from the university last year. It was tempting to go straight into a master's program; I wanted to get real-world job experience first." (A semicolon joins two related clauses together without using a period or a comma + conjunction.)

- "I graduated with honors from the university last year. It was tempting to go straight into a master's program, but [comma + conjunction] I wanted to get real-world job experience first."

Any of those three sentences would be fine.

4. Run-on sentences. This problem is similar to the comma splice except that instead of two or more complete thoughts (i.e., independent clauses) being separated by mere commas, in a run-on there is no separating punctuation at all. This is a perfect way to cause confusion and headaches for your reader. Consider this example:

- "Poor Humpty fell off the wall he broke into a hundred pieces."

Okay, wait. So did Humpty break into a hundred pieces when he fell off the wall, or did Humpty break the wall into a hundred pieces when he fell off? Let me exert a little gut-busting effort here and insert a period to clear things up:

- "Poor Humpty fell off the wall. He broke into a hundred pieces."

There—so much better!

A semicolon would also be fine:

- "Poor Humpty fell off the wall; he broke into a hundred pieces."

(See more on semicolons above . . . and below.)

Proper punctuation makes our writing more clear and therefore aids our readers' understanding. That's its purpose.

5. Inappropriate use of the apostrophe. This is one of my pet peeve's, so later, Ill discuss it in more detail. Ill bet you cant wait! (Yes, I intended to write these sentences as they are. As a joke. What do you mean you're "not laughing"?)

Until then, here's one important no-no for apostrophes: don't use an apostrophe to make a plural (as in, "This is one of my pet peeve's." No. *Please* don't commit apostrophe abuse. Thank you.)

So, there you have it: five common punctuation errors to avoid. Happy writing!

A Punctuation Riddle: The Mysterious Semicolon

What do we do with the pesky semicolon? First, let me point out that the word itself is a closed compound: there is no hyphen in it; it's one word: *semicolon.*[24]

The semicolon is one of the most misunderstood punctuation marks. Those of us who write know that it has something to do with making a pause or a break in running text, and that

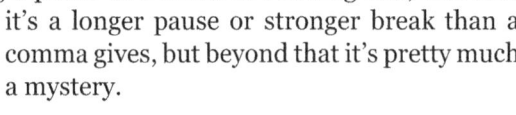

it's a longer pause or stronger break than a comma gives, but beyond that it's pretty much a mystery.

Let me try to solve the mystery. A semicolon is *most commonly* used between two independent clauses that aren't joined by a conjunction (e.g., *for, and, nor, but, or, yet, so*) where there is a closer connection between the clauses than a period indicates.

For example, let's say I want to write,

---

[24] Semicolons were discussed briefly above. This is an expansion on that discussion.

- "The woman worked at a medical clinic. Her job was to give sports physicals to school-aged children."

Those independent clauses could remain as separate sentences, but maybe I want to show a closer connection between them. I could remove the period at the end of the first sentence, replace it with a comma, and follow it with a conjunction—like this:

- "The woman worked at a medical clinic, **and** her job was to give sports physicals to school-aged children."

That would be fine. But maybe I want to give a little more sense of separation between the clauses—more separation than a comma-conjunction combo but not as much as a period. So, I use a semicolon instead:

- "The woman worked at a medical clinic; her job was to give vaccinations to school-age children."

Keep in mind that most often, dividing thoughts into distinct sentences is preferable. Use a semicolon only when the ideas in two sentences are so closely related that a less distinct break between them is needed.

A second use of semicolons is to separate independent clauses joined by a conjunction when there are multiple commas within the clauses. This is something we often see in correctly written obituaries in the newspaper. For example:

- "John Smith is survived by his wife, Susie; his children, John Smith Jr. and his wife, Betty-Boop; Sally Mae Jones and her husband, Jim Bob; and Mary (Quite Contrary) Smith; and twelve grandchildren."

These aren't the *only* uses of the semicolon; they are the most common. (Notice that I chose to use a semicolon here instead of making two separate sentences or joining the independent clauses with a comma-conjunction combo.)

Where people often mess up with the semicolon is using one instead of a colon to indicate that something is following. I see that error frequently on social media. For example,

- "Here are the things you'll need to give your true love on the twelve days of Christmas; a partridge in a pear tree, two turtledoves, three French hens . . ."

Nope, that's wrong. A colon (:) should follow *Christmas*.

Punctuation Challenge – Hyphens and Dashes

It seems that most of us don't know the difference between a hyphen and a dash. That little horizontal mark is a dash, right? End of story. Or wait—could it be a hyphen? Oh, well, whatever.

And most folks don't care. But they should because there's a difference, and well-heeled, grammatically correct writers will know what it is. In fact, there are three different little marks here, each with its own distinct use: the hyphen, the em dash, and the en dash. The following will *briefly* describe these.[25]

First, let's consider the **hyphen**, which is derived from the Greek *hypo* (under) + *hen* (one). Literally, a hyphen is "under one." Does that help? I didn't think so.

A hyphen, the shortest of the three horizontal punctuation marks we'll be talking about, has several basic uses:

(1) To avoid confusion by joining two or more words together to make compound adjectives. For example, *small-business owners* makes clear that we're talking about the owners of small businesses, not business owners who happen to be

---

[25] For a much more detailed explanation of hyphens and dashes, see June Casagrande's outstanding *The Best Punctuation Book, Period.* She devotes an entire, 27-page chapter to hyphens, and one brief chapter each to em and en dashes.

small. "Big-breakfast eaters" are folks who eat big breakfasts, not eaters of breakfast who happen to be big (although, it's possible that both may be true.). We use hyphens to clarify what we mean in these instances.

(2) Sometimes several words are hyphenated to form an adjective (e.g., *state-of-the-art sound system*). Terms like that are always hyphenated.

(3) Hyphens are used in numbers and dates (e.g., *thirty-five*; *twenty-first century*; *6-10-2021*).

Dashes differ from hyphens, and there are two types:

(1) The **em dash**—so named because it is essentially the width of the letter M—is by far the more common dash, and is used to insert clarifying information ("John's wife, Sally—his third wife—was president of the local PTA in 1975.") Sometimes, it's used like parentheses ("When it stops raining—which should happen tonight—we'll go to the grocery store.")

Note: If you are typing a paper and use dashes, there should be **no spaces** on either side of the dash. Also, two hyphens together make an em dash. Avoid using a wee little hyphen in those instances where you should be using an em dash. That is a an extremely common punctuation gaff.

(2) The **en dash** (so named because it is essentially the width of the letter N. The en dash usually means *to*, *through*, or *until*, as in "The shopping mall is open daily 9 a.m.–10 p.m.", or "The home team beat the visitors 21–7.

When using writing software, such as Microsoft Word, you can find the em and en dashes here: in the ribbon at the top, click on **Insert**, then click on **Symbol**. You may need to click on the **More Symbols** tab. Finally, in the **Special Characters** tab you will find the em and en dashes.[26]

---

[26] If you find that you use these symbols frequently (as I do), you may want to make keyboard shortcuts for them.Go to the File tab, find Options, and follow the instructions for making keyboard shortcuts.

Apostrophe Use, Misuse, and Abuse

Let's review the main uses of the apostrophe:

Possessives

- Singular nouns are made possessive with an apostrophe-*s*, even if the noun ends in -*s*: (ex. *the blog's writer*; *my boss's office*).

- Plural nouns ending in -*s* are made possessive with an apostrophe alone (ex. *the students' papers*).

- Plural nouns ending in another letter are made possessive with an apostrophe-*s* (ex. *the children's toys*).

Contractions

Use an apostrophe to form contractions. The apostrophe represents a missing letter or letters and connects (or contracts) two words together into one new word. The first sentence of this article has three contractions:

- *it's* (for *it is)*

- *you'd* (for *you would*)

- *haven't* (for *have not*)

Missing Letters or Numbers

Apostrophes may be used to represent or "stand in for" letters or numbers, similar to their use in contractions:

- *I love rock 'n' roll* (note the two apostrophes: one for the *a* and one for the *d*).

- *I'm dancin' and singin' in the rain* (the apostrophes "stand in" for the missing *g* in these words).

- *I graduated from high school in the '70s* (note: the apostrophe represents the *19*, and there is no apostrophe following the number. This is written wrong frequently).

Some Plurals

Use an apostrophe, rarely, when needed to avoid confusion:

- *Be sure to mind your* p's *and* q's.

But *Not* Most Plurals

Use only an *-s* (with no apostrophe) to form the plurals of dates, acronyms, and families:

- *The Great Depression occurred in the* 1930s.

- *The high school students took their* SATs *on Saturday.*

- *The* Garcias *invited everyone to their home for Thanksgiving.*

Avoid Apostrophe Misuse and Abuse

- Do NOT use apostrophe's to make word's plural (as in this sentence).

- Do NOT use an apostrophe in the adjectival pronoun *its*:

Wrong: *The dog is chasing it's tail.*
Correct: *The dog is chasing its tail.*[27]

Random Apostrophe Placement in Proper Names

What category do we place this under? Is it clever apostrophe use, unfortunate misuse, or strange abuse? You tell me.

I have noted what is apparently a peculiar trend of late to include apostrophes in the middle of proper names, such as *An'drew* or *Mar'ia* or *Hamil'ton*. I must confess this confuses me. I can't see any actual purpose for the seemingly randomly placed apostrophe, and therefore I've concluded that it serves

---

[27] See separate essay in this book.

merely as a kind of euonymus appellation akin to a hood ornament—something to make folks pause and think, "Well, that's . . . unique/interesting/fancy." I don't know for sure; if you do, let me know. Seriously.

Chapter 4
A Grammar Miscellany

Grammar is not just a pain in the ass; it's the pole you grab to get your thoughts up on their feet and walking. – Stephen King, *On Writing*

Between You and I, We've Got a Problem

In this essay, I want to talk about me. No, I don't mean me, Dean, I mean the objective pronoun *me* versus the nominative pronoun *I*. One of the most common errors in speech and writing is to use *I* where *me* should be.

Here's the **general rule** in the simplest terms: Use *I* as the subject of a sentence or clause and *me* as the object of a sentence or clause.

Let me give some **examples** of the incorrect use of these pronouns:

- "People gave my wife and I four toasters for wedding presents." (incorrect)

- "One of the best things to happen to Gary and I is that we became best friends." (incorrect)

Here's why both are incorrect: the pronoun *I* is virtually always used in the nominative case, as the *subject* of a sentence or clause, not the *object*. The objective pronoun is *me*. Replace *I* with *me* in both sentences:

- "People gave my wife and *me* four toasters for wedding presents." (correct)

- "One of the best things to happen to Gary and *me* is that we became best friends." (correct)

Here's an easy test to use when you're not sure:

In your mind, take out the "[other person's name] and" and see how it sounds. Let's try it with our examples.

- "People gave my wife and I four toasters for wedding presents."

Which becomes:

- "People gave I four toasters for wedding presents."

Doesn't sound right, does it? Nope. But "People gave my wife and me four toasters" is better. It's definitely too many toasters, but grammatically, it's better.

How about this one:

- "One of the best things to happen to Gary and I is that we became best friends."

Which becomes:

- "One of the best things to happen to I is that we became best friends."

Uh-uh. Just doesn't sound right. Make it "Gary and me" and it sounds muy bueno!

So even if you forget the rule about nominative *I* and objective *me*, if you remember that simple test, you'll get the *I-me* thing right most of the time.

How about an example of using the nominative *I* correctly?

- "My wife and I gave the newlyweds a toaster for a wedding gift." ("My wife and I" is the subject in this sentence and therefore is correct.)

Subjective case "I" vs. objective case "me" – An extremely "popular" grammatical error occurs when these two are confused. An entire essay can be devoted to it, but here's an example to keep in mind: when listing couples, families, or small groups, be sure to use the subjective "I" in sentences like this:

"Those who attended the meeting were Bobby, Carol, Teddy, and Alice; Juan and Maria; and Betty and I."

Why not "Betty and me"? Because the intent of the list is to make all the names the subject of the sentence (i.e., "Bobby, Carol, Teddy, and Alice [attended the meeting]; Juan and Maria [attended the meeting]; and Betty and I [attended the meeting]." Try the "sounds good/bad test" on "Betty and me": "Betty and me attended the meeting." Nope! Doesn't sound good.

Between you and me, let's fix the title of this essay: It's "between you and me," **not** "between you and I," which is simply wrong. *You* and *me* are both objects of the preposition *between*. Make sense? Of course!

Watch Out for Misplaced Modifiers

A modifier is a word or phrase that describes something. A modifier at the beginning of a sentence is considered "misplaced" when it doesn't match up with what follows, which can cause confusion for your reader. For example, I recently received an email from an organization I support financially. Here's how it began, "Dear Dean: As a faithful supporter of our organization, we are requesting your participation in a special research project."

The modifier there is "faithful supporter." But who is that? Is it "Dean" or is it "we"? Grammatically, as this sentence is written, "we" (the organization) are the "faithful supporter" of the organization. Huh? That's silly, of course, and doesn't make sense—I knew they were referring to me—but if we take it at face value, that's exactly what they are saying. "As a **faithful supporter, we** are requesting . . ."

Yes, I knew who they were talking about—that I was the faithful supporter, and they were asking for my help—but I had to pause for a second to mentally make that connection. When we begin a sentence with "as," "like," or "unlike," we need to be extra careful about what comes next.

Maybe this would have been better: "Dear Dean: Because you are a faithful supporter of our organization, would you be willing to help us out with a special research project?"

Doesn't that seem a bit clearer?

Here's a snippet from another email I received, this time from the publisher of the local newspaper:

"Dear Dean, As a highly valued former subscriber of The Newspaper, we thought you might appreciate a sneak peek at some of the things we'll be covering over the next few months that we don't want you to miss."

In this case, the misplaced modifier identifies The Newspaper as the "highly valued, former subscriber." Here's a simple clarification: "Because you are a valued former subscriber . . . we thought you might . . ."

Wow! And from a newspaper publisher. He needs a copyeditor!

Here's another example: "Amid the ongoing investigation of his wife's financial affairs, Attorney General Smith had a secret closed-door meeting with former Governor Horton."

Wait, what? *Whose* "private email server"? As it reads, it's Attorney General Smith's wife's private email server. But, uh, I don't think that was the intended meaning. The phrase "his wife's" is the misplaced modifier.

It could have been clarified with a simple rewrite: "Amid the ongoing investigation of Mrs. Johnson's financial affairs, Attorney General Smith . . ."

Watch out for misplaced modifiers.

Zapping Three Grammar Myths

#1: It is okay to begin a sentence with a conjunction!

According to Merriam-Webster's Dictionary, a conjunction is "a word that joins together sentences, clauses, phrases, or words." The seven most common conjunctions are *for, and, nor, but, or, yet,* and *so.* (So you can recall them, remember the acronym FANBOYS.)

Edward Good, in *Who's (Oops) Whose Grammar Book Is This Anyway*, writes, "Never start a sentence with a conjunction. Poppycock! Not only can you start sentences with a conjunction, but you must—if you ever want to become a good writer, that is."[28] Bill Walsh cautions, "Starting a sentence with a conjunction is a literary device that can be overused. And it can be annoying. But there's nothing inherently evil about it."[29]

#2: Go ahead and split your infinitives!

An infinitive is composed of *to* plus a verb (e.g., *to eat, to study, to go*). Splitting an infinitive is to put a word (or words) **between** the *to* and the verb, as in "to **clearly** see." Garner says, "Although few armchair grammarians seem to know it, some split infinitives are regarded as perfectly proper."[30] As far back as 1916, professor James C. Fernald wrote, "Many grammarians hold that an adverb should never come between the *to* of the infinitive and the verb for; as, *to* faithfully *study.* Others give this usage a qualified approval. It is found in some good authors, and is becoming very prevalent."[31] Bill Walsh goes as far as to say that he knows of "no usage authorities who believe that split

---

[28] Good 2002, 157.
[29] Walsh, *The Elephants of Style* 2004, 67.
[30] *Garner's Modern English Usage*, Fourth Edition 2016, 767.
[31] Fernald 1916, 84.

infinitives are always wrong. . . . More often than not . . . infinitives are better split."[32]

How do you know when it's okay to split an infinitive? Let your ear tell you. Paula LaRocque says, "We are right to split an infinitive when the unsplit version is clumsy or unclear."[33] For example, to quote Captain James T. Kirk: "To boldly go where no man has gone before." The infinitive is split, but it sounds so right.

#3: And while you're at it, feel free to end your sentence with a preposition!

Prepositions are words like *about, from, in, onto, of, to,* and *with.* Edward Good says that "great writers have been ending sentences and clauses with prepositions for centuries.[34] For example, "I pushed my friend down the steps after recess. What was I thinking of?" It would just sound too stuffy to write, "Of what was I thinking?" Grammarians recommend that you not overdo this in formal writing, but again—if it makes sense and sounds right, indulge yourself.

There, isn't it liberating to be set free from three grammar myths in one sitting?

---

[32] Walsh, Ibid, 64.
[33] LaRocque 2003, 214.
[34] Good 2002, 171.

In Formal Writing, When Should You Use the Ampersand (&) in Place of "And"?

The short answer to the above question is . . . *never.*

Or at least *rarely.*

The longer answer is that the ampersand (&) is used in some instances as the legitimate abbreviation for the word *and*, and is appropriate in notes, bibliographies, and tabular matter. Further, when it appears in the formal name of a company or logo, it is always appropriate. For example, AT&T, Johnson & Johnson, JPMorgan Chase & Co., and PG&E.[35] Occasionally, it is used as a space-saving or stylistic device in the title of a work, such as *Nothing About Baseball Is Trivial: Essential Terms, Rules, Stats & History for Fans and Wannabe Fans.*[36]

Style guides, such as *The Associated Press Stylebook*, expressly state that "the ampersand should not otherwise be used in place of *and*."[37]

However, when you do use it, here are a few guidelines to remember: (1) If writing a sentence containing serial (or Oxford) commas, you would normally insert that comma before the *and*; but (2) the comma is *omitted* when using an ampersand; (3) when the ampersand appears in a company initialism (such as AT&T), there is no space before and after the & symbol.

Let's again look at the above book title example: *Essential Terms, Rules, Stats & History for Fans and Wannabe Fans.* (Note, no comma before &). Otherwise, include the serial

---

[35] That's Pacific Gas and Electric for my non-West Coast readers.
[36] How's that for a sneaky way to slip in the title of my first book. Don't ask me why I didn't use an ampersand for the second *and*. Just . . . don't ask. Thanks.
[37] *AP Stylebook* 2017, 17.

comma: *Essential Terms, Rules, Stats, and History for Fans and Wannabe Fans.*

To reiterate, the ampersand should be avoided in almost all instances of formal writing. Instead, spell it out: *a-n-d.*

I hope this is clear. If so, go forth & conquer! (I mean, go forth *and* conquer!)

Regular vs. Irregular Verbs

Verbs give life and movement to our writing. We should study verbs and learn to use them effectively.

What is a verb? A verb "shows the performance or occurrence of an action or the existence of a condition or a state of being, such as an emotion."[38]

Verbs are either *regular* or *irregular*. What's the difference? A **regular** verb does not change form in its past or past participle tenses—the base word remains the same and *-ed* or *-d* are added to make it past: e.g., "I *look* out the window; I *looked* out the window this morning; I have *looked* out the window all day." An **irregular** verb, on the other had, does change form in its past tense and past participle: e.g., I *give*, I *gave*, I have *given*; I *sink*, I *sank*, I had *sunk*; you *do*, you *did*, you have *done*; we *win*, we *won*, we have *won*.

You have probably noticed that young children who are just learning to talk will instinctively treat all verbs as regular in forming past and past participles. For example, *go* becomes *goed*, *see* becomes *seed*, *sing* becomes *singed*, *eat* becomes *eated*, etc., until they learn that irregular verbs change their past/past participle forms.

I wish that we acquired this knowledge by osmosis—and in a sense we do, if by "osmosis" we mean that youngsters learn and become adept at irregular verbs by means of the environment they grew up in. But even those of us blessed to have been nurtured in a vocabulary-rich home are challenged with some forms of irregular verbs, and in the English language, there are fewer than 270. Therefore I have included the following list of the approximately 100 most common irregular verbs.[39]

---

38 Garner, *The Chicago Guide to Grammar, Usage, and Punctuation* 2016, 71.
39 Source: https://www.e-grammar.org/irregular-verbs/

Base Form	Past Simple	Past Participle
be	was/were	been
bear	bore	born
beat	beat	beaten
become	became	become
begin	began	begun
bet	bet	bet
bite	bit	bitten
blow	blew	blown
broadcast	broadcast	broadcast
break	broke	broken
bring	brought	brought
build	built	built
burn	burnt	burnt
buy	bought	bought
can	could	-----
catch	caught	caught
choose	chose	chosen
come	came	come
cost	cost	cost
cut	cut	cut
do	did	done
draw	drew	drawn
dream	dreamt	dreamt
drink	drank	drunk
drive	drove	driven
eat	ate	eaten
fall	fell	fallen
feed	fed	fed
feel	felt	felt
fight	fought	fought
find	found	found
fly	flew	flown
forget	forgot	forgotten
freeze	froze	frozen
get	got	got
give	gave	given
go	went	gone
grow	grew	grown
hang	hung	hung
have	had	had
hear	heard	heard
hide	hid	hidden
hit	hit	hit
hold	held	held
hurt	hurt	hurt

Base Form	Past Simple	Past Participle
keep	kept	kept
know	knew	known
lead	led	led
learn	learnt	learnt
leave	left	left
lend	lent	lent
let	let	let
lie	lay	lain
lose	lost	lost
make	made	made
mean	meant	meant
meet	met	met
pay	paid	paid
put	put	put
read	read	read
ride	rode	ridden
ring	rang	rung
rise	rose	risen
run	ran	run
say	said	said
see	saw	seen
sell	sold	sold
send	sent	sent
set	set	set
shoot	shot	shot
show	showed	shown
shrink	shrank	shrunk
shut	shut	shut
sing	sang	sung
sink	sank	sunk
sit	sat	sat
sleep	slept	slept
speak	spoke	spoken
spend	spent	spent
stand	stood	stood
steal	stole	stolen
stick	stuck	stuck
stink	stank	stunk
swim	swam	swum
understand	understood	understood
take	took	taken
teach	taught	taught
tell	told	told
think	thought	thought
throw	threw	thrown

Base Form	Past Simple	Past Participle
wake	woke	woken
wear	wore	worn
win	won	won
write	wrote	written

"Irregular verbs are sometimes called 'strong' verbs because they seem to form the past tense from their own resources, without calling an ending to their assistance. The regular verbs are sometimes called 'weak' verbs because they cannot form the past tense without the aid of the ending (most often -ed.")
– Bryan A. Garner, *Garner's Modern English Usage*

The Bare-Bones Basics of Sentence-Writing

In this age of social media that has turned all of us into writers (or, ahem, "writers"), the basic unit of written communication remains the same—the sentence.

Obviously, you can find literally hundreds (maybe thousands) of books on writing that provide much more detail than I intend to provide here. So I'll make this as quick and painless as possible.

A sentence, in its basic form, is a group of words that can stand alone to express a complete thought—sometimes called an **independent clause**. An independent clause contains at least one subject and one verb (**S-V**). That's called a **simple sentence**. "The boy runs" is a simple sentence.

Many simple sentences contain a subject, a verb, and an object of the verb (**S-V-O**). For example, "Washington (subject) chopped down (verb) the cherry tree (object)." There is just one independent clause in a simple sentence.

A **compound sentence** contains two (or more) independent clauses. E.g., "The home team was losing and the fans were restless." Notice that two complete thoughts are joined by the little word *and*, which serves as a **coordinating conjunction**. When two independent clauses are closely related in thought they can be separated by a semicolon: "The home team was losing; the fans were restless." Or you can simply make two short sentences: "The home team was losing. The fans were restless."

A **complex sentence** contains a single independent clause and two or more dependent clauses. A **dependent clause** cannot stand alone; it is dependent on other words in the sentence to make a complete thought and is often preceded by "because." E.g., "The fans were restless because the home team was losing." Note that "because the home team was losing" is not a stand-alone (or independent) clause; the word *because* is dependent on more information to make sense. You could also write the sentence, "Because the home team was losing, the fans were restless."

Finally, we have the **compound-complex sentence**, which contains two or more independent clauses and at least one dependent clause. E.g., "Because the home team was losing, the fans were restless and the players were frustrated." Note that a second independent clause ("the players were frustrated") was added to our above example, joined by the coordinating conjunction *and*.

To summarize, then, there are four basic types of sentences: the simple, the compound, the complex, and the compound-complex.

Now, there are exceptions to this "rule." At times, a simple interjection ("Ah!" "Wahoo!" "Oy!" "Ouch!") can serve as a sentence; at other times, a short phrase is perfectly fine ("Got it." "Way to go!" "Outstanding meal!" "Big deal!")

The single best piece of advice I can give to improve your sentences is to keep them short. This will often enable you to use less punctuation, which is a bugaboo for a lot of people. However, my single best piece of advice regarding punctuation is this: use it. End your sentences with the appropriate terminal punctuation (i.e., periods, question marks, or exclamation marks).[40]

If you want to be a writer, you must do two things above all others: read a lot and write a lot. There's no way around these two things . . . no shortcut.

— Stephen King, *On Writing*

---

[40] But please . . . use exclamation marks sparingly. Some people write

Subjects and Verbs Must Agree

When I copyedit documents, one of the most common grammar issues I find (besides punctuation problems) is subject-verb agreement difficulties.

In simplest terms, in any sentence, verbs must agree with their noun and pronoun subjects in number, whether singular or plural. **Look for the subject of the sentence and don't be distracted by intervening prepositional phrases**, which may be the most common cause of subject-verb agreement problems. Consider the following **example**:

"The box of chocolates (*has/have*) fallen on the floor." The correct verb is *has*, although many writers would mistakenly write *have*. How can you be sure? Trust your ear. Remove the prepositional phrase (*of chocolates*) and hear what makes sense: "The box [singular subject] **has** fallen [singular verb] on the floor."

Another example: "The main argument of the defense attorneys (*is/are*) that the defendant wasn't anywhere near the scene of the crime that day." Remove the prepositional phrase (*of the defense attorneys*) and what remains? "The main argument [singular subject] **is** [singular verb] that the defendant wasn't anywhere near the scene of the crime that day."[41]

---

[41] Admittedly, this only scratches the surface of this crucial topic. For further study, I recommend any of the following works, which can be found in the bibliography: Lester and Larry 2005, 123-138; Hacker 1985, 126-136; Strunk Jr. and White 2009, 9-11; Thurman 2003, 46-52; Garner, *The Chicago Guide to Grammar, Usage, and Punctuation* 2016, 115-120; Straus 2014, 3-7.

"My husband and I's Vacation"

Ouch! This one hurts. Really badly. Instead it should be, "My husband's and my vacation." Here's the trick: remove one of the phrases—either "my husband and" or "I's vacation"—and listen to it. Does it sound okay to say, "My husband vacation"? or, "I's vacation"? No. Neither sounds right. Instead, we would say, "My husband's vacation" or "my vacation." Much better. To put it all together, then, we would say, "My husband**'s** and **my** vacation."

Here's another example: "Take a look at my wife and I's new car." How to fix it? Follow the above pattern: "Take a look at my wife**'s** and **my** new car."

Voila! Perfect grammar.

Writing is thinking made visible. It is the messy business of listening for, exploring, and discovering what we know or mean or thought we meant when we started. It involves rehearsing, mapping, discarding, revising, shaping, weighing, and negotiating with meaning. It begins before we start, and all of our experience has a say in what happens.

We write in the shower, in the car, in the middle of dreams, and often while our hands are at rest.
We fight the white page, the empty screen.
The mind is at work, but the stomach participates, as do the hairs on the backs of our necks.
We may stop; but we never finish.

As soon as we see our crafted words in print we scowl, "I wish I had it to do over again. It isn't right."

– Chris Paulis, "A Christmas Carol of Language Writing"

Me, Myself, and I: Using These Pronouns Correctly

"Would you like some ice cream?" asked Mother.

"Yippee! All three of us would!" cried six-year-old Dean.

"Three? I only see you."

"Oh, no, there are three: me, myself, and I. That means three bowls of ice cream!"

"Oh," she said, coughing once and rolling her eyes.

Thus began Dean's disastrous, short-lived career as a stand-up comedian.

But seriously, folks—when do we use the pronouns *me*, *myself*, and *I*? Specifically, how do we properly use **reflexive** pronouns (*myself, yourself, herself, ourselves*, etc.)? Are they just another way of saying *I/me*, *you*, *her*, and *us*?

I won't leave you in suspense: the answer is NO. Here's a chart showing all reflexive (and intensive) pronouns:

	Reflexive Pronouns	
Person	**Singular**	**Plural**
First person	myself	ourselves
Second person	yourself	yourselves
Third person	himself	themselves
	herself	
	itself	

Reflexive pronouns show that an action was performed by someone on himself or herself (or by something on itself). Ex.: "**I** made the cherry pie **myself**." "**Mary** gave **herself** a pep talk." "The **oven** cleans **itself**."

Intensive pronouns (the same list as above) are used for emphasis. They let the reader know that an action was performed by or directed toward only the person or thing that the pronoun refers to. The distinction between intensive and reflexive pronouns is often subtle, and in the interest of avoiding confusion, I'll leave it at that.

Many folks misuse reflexive pronouns. For example, I'm currently reading a novel by a highly successful author. In the introduction he wrote, "The nasty side of myself wanted to answer that [question] . . ." A few pages later, he wrote, "Fiction . . . always has the possibility of being about ourself." Both of those are nonstandard usages. He is using reflexive pronouns where he should have used personal pronouns. Since I usually read with a pencil in hand, I crossed out the reflexive pronouns *myself* and *ourself* and in the margin scrawled "*My* nasty side" or "The nasty side of *me*" and "the possibility of being about *us*" in the margins.

So why are those wrong (or, if you flinch at the word *wrong*, I can use the term *nonstandard*), and what's the big deal? Here's the big deal: a reflexive pronoun always needs an antecedent (the noun it's taking the place of) that is the same person or thing. If there is a *myself* in a sentence, there must be an *I* as its antecedent: "**I** bought **myself** a new car." If there is a *yourself*, there must be a *you* as its antecedent: "**You** did **yourself** a favor when you changed into that dress." If there is an ourself (which is wrong anyway—the correct plural form is *ourselves*) there must be an antecedent—usually a *we*. "**We** helped **ourselves** to some cake and ice cream."

It would be incorrect to say, "My wife and myself went to the movies last weekend." Since reflexive pronouns are to be used when the object reflects or bends back (thus is reflexive) on the subject, this won't work. In this sentence, *myself* is part of the subject and is therefore wrong. Reflexive pronouns cannot function as the subject of a clause or sentence. The correct pronoun here would be *I*: "My wife and I (compound subject) went to the movies last weekend."

Let me leave you with a couple more examples of incorrect and correct uses of personal and reflexive pronouns:

- "The chef cooked a gourmet meal for myself last week." (Incorrect.) The reflexive pronoun myself must refer back to an antecedent. There is none.

- "I cooked a gourmet meal for myself last week." (Correct. A lie, but grammatically correct because *myself* refers to its antecedent, *I*.)

- "Curry threw the ball to myself and I dunked it." (Incorrect. Again, there's no antecedent for *myself*, so a reflexive pronoun is inappropriate.)

- "Curry threw the ball to me, and I dunked it." (Correct. The objective personal pronoun *me* is appropriate; no reflexive pronoun is needed.)

Isn't English grammar fun? (If you disagree, please don't write *myself* a nasty comment.)

Adjective Ordering

Here's one of those lovely little ancient "laws" of English that we all seem to obey instinctively but couldn't explain if our lives depended on it. Well, maybe *you* could, but I only recently learned it.

It has to do with how we line up multiple adjectives in a sentence. We say things like, "She was wearing a new red silk dress."

Or "The old gray mare, she ain't what she used to be."

Or "I liked the fantastic big old yellow bus that took me to school every day."

What's this "lovely little ancient law of English" I'm talking about? We call it the Order of Adjectives Law,[42] and it goes like this:

1. **Opinion**: pretty, horrible, lovely

2. **Size**: huge, tiny, big, little

3. **Age**: old, young, new

4. **Shape**: round, square, triangular

5. **Color**: blue, red, yellow, gray

6. **Origin**: British, American, French, Mid-Western

7. **Material**: glass, wooden, silk, plastic

8. **Purpose** (i.e., what it's used for): writing, shopping, school, church, dancing

Notice, the first letter of these words spell the fabulous acronym OSASCOMP.

As Mark Forsythe points out, "You can have a lovely little old rectangular green French silver whittling knife. But if you

---

[42] Since I capitalized those words, this thing has to be pretty special.

mess with that word order in the slightest you'll sound like a maniac."[43]

That may be a bit of an exaggeration, but referring back to my earlier examples, if we'd said, "She was wearing a silk red new dress," or "The gray old mare . . .", or "the old big yellow fantastic bus," people would at least look at you funny.

I-A-O Order

While we're on this subject of word orders, here's another oddity to think about. Why do we automatically seem to say hip-hop (instead of hop-hip), or tick-tock (instead of tock-tick), or flim-flam (instead of flam-flim)? Why does Mary Poppins say "spit-spot" and not "spot-spit"? Hmm?

It's because when we repeat a word with a different vowel, the order is always I-A-O: bish-bash-bosh! Zip-zap-zoom! Flippity, flappity, floppity! Tic, tac, toe. Who's afraid of the big, bad wolf? (We wouldn't dream of saying, "bad, big wolf," would we?) And those little oddments we display on our shelves are knickknacks, not knackknicks.

Politicians may flip-flop on a matter, but they can't flop-flip. Getting even is giving tit-for-tat, not tat-for-tit.

Is there a word for this "law"? Yes, there is. It's called *ablaut reduplication*.[44]

So now you know.

---

[43] Forsyth 2014, 39.
[44] Forsyth 2014, 40. MW-11 defines *ablaut* as a "systematic variation of vowels in the same root or affix or in related roots or affixes . . . as in *sing, sang, sung, song*."

Good, Better, or Best? Using the Correct Form of Comparison Words

What form do adjectives and adverbs take when we make comparisons between two or more people, places, things, or ideas. We say things like, "My son is *taller* than my daughter"; "This winter in California is the *driest* in decades"; "The Super Bowl was the *most terrible* one in recent history, and maybe the *worst* ever (unless you're a Seahawks fan)."

Comparison Forms

Here's how we categorize comparison forms of adjectives and adverbs:

The **general rule** is that one-syllable adjectives become comparative by adding *-er* and superlative by adding *-est*. This is true of many two-syllable adjectives and adverbs as well, such as *lively →livelier →liveliest*.

Sometimes, we add *more* or *most*, as in *agile →more agile →most agile*. When in doubt, consult a good dictionary.

Adjectives of more than two syllables and adverbs ending in *-ly* usually form their comparative and superlative degrees by using *more* and *most*.

For example: *terrible →more terrible →most terrible*; or *delightful →more delightful →most delightful*.

On the following page is a chart showing examples of the **degree of comparison** basics. (Note that the "positive" degree simply makes a statement about a person, place, thing, or idea.)

71

POSITVE (adjective or adverb)	COMPARATIVE (comparing two)	SUPERLATIVE (comparing more than two)
Tall	Taller	Tallest
Dry	Drier	Driest
Terrible	More Terrible	Most Terrible
Bad	Worse	Worst
Good	Better	Best
Young	Younger	Youngest
Old	Older	Oldest
Many	More	Most

A Common Mistake: Using the Superlative Instead of the Comparative

Now, here's a common mistake involving the use of the superlative; you will find it in both spoken and written communication. Often, when someone is referring to two people, whether a couple, a parent's two kids, or whatever, they incorrectly use the superlative instead of the comparative degree.

For example, a father with two (and only two) children might say, "My *oldest* child is going off to college this fall." Consulting the chart above, what should he have said? That's right: "My *older* (or *elder*) child is going off to college this fall." Or a mother with two (and only two) daughters might say, "My youngest daughter talks so much, I think she was vaccinated with a phonograph needle."[45] Aside from making a veiled insult, the mother should have used which comparison adjective? Yes: "My *younger* daughter." When there are *more* than two, we use the superlative form: *oldest, youngest, best, strongest, most fantastic, most intelligent,* and so forth.

I hope today is more wonderful than yesterday—maybe even the most wonderful day of the year![46]

---

[45] That's an old Groucho Marx joke. Hey, it was funny in 1933!
[46] Sources consulted for this essay: Thurman 2003 and Warriner 1988.

Four Simple Ways to Cut Out Fluff So Your Writing Flows Better

Every word we write should be doing some work in the sentence. Often, however, we inject far too much fluff in our writing. What are "fluff words"? They are expressions that add to our word count, but not to the flow, clarity, or overall appeal of our writing. They tend to weaken our writing.

Here are some tips:

Limit Qualifiers

Do we ever have to write *sort of, probably, likely,* or *possibly?* Probably not.[47] Consider the following sentence:

"You will likely be a better writer if you cut out the qualifiers." Now try it without likely: "You will be a better writer if you cut out the qualifiers." It's better, right?

An exception: Certain types of writing—academic writing, for example—often require the use of qualifiers and expressions of tentativeness to suggest that the data or conclusions are not definitive, that further research is needed. That's all right, of course—but it's one of the reasons why academic writing is typically about as exciting as the Valley of Dry Bones.

Discard Intensifiers

The most common intensifier is *very.*[48] "I like you very much." "This is a very good book." "He's a very good writer." *Very* in these instances isn't needed. It's almost never needed.

The next time you draft an email, a paper for school, or a business letter, try to keep *very* out of it.

Allegedly Mark Twain wrote this about *very:*

---

[47] I just wanted to see if you were paying attention. Let me replace "probably not" with "No." It's simple, clear, to the point.
[48] *Very* is also sometimes considered a qualifier. (See above.)

SUBSTITUTE 'DAMN' EVERY TIME YOU'RE INCLINED TO WRITE 'VERY'; YOUR EDITOR WILL DELETE IT AND THE WRITING WILL BE JUST AS IT SHOULD BE.

Remove Redundancies

A redundancy is a needless or superfluous repetition. If you can cut it out without losing information, it's a redundancy. I could list hundreds of examples, but I'll give you just one that I see all the time, and it drives me up the wall. It's the phrase "including but not limited to." The word *including* implies that what follows does not constitute all the possibilities; that it is a representative list. The phrase *not limited to* is therefore redundant. It's almost never needed. You may safely omit it from your writing lexicon. You are welcome.

Throw Out "Throwaway" Words

I taught a graduate-level class at a local university for several semesters and was always surprised at the generally weak writing reflected in the papers I assigned students. For example, almost every student would include throwaway words when describing interviews they had conducted with local educators and community leaders. "Ms. Sally was an amazing person"; "Dr. Jones provided awesome information." I would circle words like *amazing* and *awesome* and write, "This is a throwaway word that tells me nothing about your interview subject. It's an empty space-filler." We may use them frequently in casual speech, but we should avoid them in formal writing.

However, recalling Orwell's advice, "Break any of these rules sooner than say anything outright barbarous."

Curing Bloated Writing

A city mayor recently unveiled a new fiscal-year city budget proposal that called for more than a billion dollars and would include increases in funding for police, fire, parks, and road repairs.

The police chief made the following statement for the press: "This budget is a healthy budget for public safety. It is not where we need to be at some point in time in the future, but it is what we are able to get to at this point in time."

That's a good example of bloated sentence construction. Concision produces clarity, but government officials aren't typically given to concise and clear communication. Let's consider how to revise this bloated, 40-word sentence.

First, a principle: The phrase *at this point in time* should almost always be reduced to *now* or eliminated entirely. So let's try it out:

"This budget is a healthy budget for public safety. It is not where we need to be in the future, but it is what we are able to get to now."

That shortened it to thirty-one words. Better.

Can we take out more? Of course! We may need to do some rewriting, but that's normal, not exceptional. Here's a possibility:

"This is a healthy budget for public safety. Although it's not where we need to be in the future, it's a good step in that direction."

Down to twenty-six words. Much better. And what makes it better is not merely brevity but careful syntax so that each word counts.

The Team Romp?

A front-page headline in the local newspaper this morning reads, "U.S. Men's Basketball Team Romp Past China." Kudos to the U.S. men's team for romping away in your first game of these Olympics, steamrolling easily over the Chinese team 119-62. But thanks, local newspaper, for reminding us that subject-verb agreement is not always so easy. It should have read, "The U.S. Team **Romps** Past China."

Nouns that denote an aggregate of individuals or things are called collective nouns and are grammatically singular, which means they take the singular form of the verb. Common examples include *flock, herd, group, family,* and *team.* We would say, "The flock of geese **is** flying overhead"; "The green group **challenges** the blue group to a sales contest"; and "The family that **prays** together **stays** together

There are exceptions and nuances to this rule. For example, when the group is spoken of as a collection of individuals, the plural form of the verb is used, as in, "When the basketball team **plays** next, I hope **they win.** "In the first part of the sentence, *team* is a collective noun, therefore we use the singular form *plays.* In the second part, the emphasis is placed on the individuals, and therefore we hope *they* (the individuals who comprise the team) *win* (the plural form of the verb). This sounds complicated, but it's something we all get correct without thinking about it.

Suffice it to say that collective nouns are singular nouns and, as such, take singular forms of the verb.

And then, not to confuse you, there's the British usage. In British English, words like *team* or *family* are always treated as plural: "The family are traveling home to Nottingham for the holidays this year." "The team face off against China."

And may the best team win.

Commonly Used (and Misused) Latinate Abbreviations in American English

Latinate abbreviations (i.e., abbreviations of Latin expressions used in English) can serve as useful tools to enhance our writing. Or, if improperly used, they can detract from our writing—and reflect poorly on the writer. Here are some of the most common Latinate abbreviations, their meanings, and notes on their usage. Notice in particular the placement of the periods.

etc.

Et cetera, abbreviated *etc.*, means "and so forth" (literally, "and others of the same kind"). Note three things about this abbreviation: (1) It is *etc.*, not *ect.*, and it is *not* pronounced *eck-cetera*; (2) It is not "*and* etc.," (which would literally be "*and* so forth"—that's redundant); and (3) *etc.* should be used sparingly in formal writing because it's a vague term that can make the writer seem lazy—it places the burden on the reader to imagine what specifically the writer is referring to. When you must use it in formal writing, it should be in a phrase enclosed in parentheses.

e.g.

Exempli grata, abbreviated *e.g.*, means "for example." Note three things about its use: (1) it is always followed by a comma[49]: *The vendor on the corner is selling flowers for Mother's Day (e.g., red and yellow roses and white and pink carnations)*; (2) in formal writing, it should be used in parenthetical statements (as in the previous sentence). In the main text it is better to use words like "such as" or "for

---

[49] Of course, there are occasional exceptions, but for the most part, this "always followed by a comma" rule applies. However, in British English, *e.g.* (like *i.e.*) is typically *not* followed by a comma.

example"; (3) be careful not to confuse it with *i.e.*, which means something quite different.

i.e.

Id est, abbreviated *i.e.*, means "that is." Note three things about its use: (1) Like e.g., it is always followed by a comma: *The vendor on the corner is selling something almost every mother wants on Mother's Day (i.e., flowers).*; (2) like e.g., it is preferable to use *i.e.* in parenthetical expressions rather than in the main text; (3) be careful not to confuse it with *e.g.*, which means something quite different.

et al.

Et alii, abbreviated *et al.*, means "and others" (referring to people). Note three things about its use: (1) a period follows *al* because it is an abbreviation of *alii*, while *et* is the full Latin word "and"; (2) Be careful not to place the period—or worse, a comma—after either *et* or *al*; (3) it is preferable to use *et al.* in parenthetical expressions and in footnotes/end notes rather than in the main text, where it's better to spell out "and others" or "and the others."

One caveat:[50] none of the above Latinate abbreviations is italicized in text (despite their appearance as such in this essay).

---

[50] A "caveat" is literally a *warning* or a *word of caution.*

Chapter 5
Fun With Words

When you come to a fork in the road, take it.
– Yogi Berra (attributed)

Punography

One night a Viking named Rudolph the Red was looking out the window when he said, "It's going to rain." His wife asked, "How do you know?" He replied, "Because Rudolph the Red knows rain, dear."[51]

What is a pun? At its most basic, "a pun is a joke that makes a play on words. Puns rely on words that are similar in spelling, sound or meaning to make their listener laugh."[52]

Types of Puns

Puns are also known as *paronomasia*, a rhetorical device that uses the dual meanings of a word to achieve an effect. Following are the more common types of puns.

1. Homophonic Puns

When your pun relies on the way words sound alike but have different meanings and spellings, it's a homophonic pun.

Examples of homophonic puns are:

---

[51] I stole this from a "meme" shared by a friend on Facebook, who stole it from someone else.
[52] This quote and much of the following material are taken from https://examples.yourdictionary.com/examples-of-puns.html.

- A bicycle can't stand on its own because it is **two-tired**.

- A pessimist's blood type is always **B-negative**.

- My friend Jack claims he can communicate with vegetables. Jack and the beans talk.

2. Homographic Puns

Homographic puns are also known as heteronymic ("same name") puns. They're funny because they're true in both interpretations of the word, and they are best understood when read.

Homographic pun examples include:

- After hours of waiting for the bowling alley to open, we finally **got the ball rolling**.

- Always trust a glue salesman. They tend to **stick** to their word.

- If you don't pay your exorcist, you will get **repossessed**.

3. Zeugmas

A zeugma is a pun that "involves one verb and more than one object, one of which is unanticipated."

Example: "She tossed back her cloak, her hair, and a jigger of whiskey. When he saw her standing in the rain, he opened his umbrella and his heart."[53]

4. Compound Puns

Compound puns include two punny words in one statement, or they rely on the sound of two words blended together to make the joke.

Examples of compound puns are:

---

[53] LaRocque 2003, 160.

- One hundred **hares** have escaped the zoo, so police are **combing** the area.

- Did you hear about the lumberjack who couldn't **hack** it? They gave him the **axe**.

Fun Pun Examples

- She had a photographic memory but never **developed** it.

- I was struggling to figure out how lightning works, but then **it struck me**.

- I've been to the dentist many times, so I know the **drill**.

- The other day I held the door open for a clown. I thought it was a nice **jester**.

- A chicken crossing the road is truly **poultry in motion**.

- A boiled egg every morning is hard to **beat**.

- Two antennas met on a roof, fell in love and got married. The ceremony wasn't much, but the **reception** was brilliant!

Puns in Quotes

Comedians and writers use puns all the time in their acts and writing. Examples of puns in quotes from famous people include these:

- "Hanging is too good for a man who makes puns; he should be drawn and quoted." – Fred Allen

- "Denial ain't just a river in Egypt." – Mark Twain

- "I saw a documentary on how ships are kept together. Riveting!" – Stewart Francis

Puns in Headlines and Advertising

Editors and advertisers often employ puns in their copy. They get readers' attention because they often have to read it a second time to get the meaning. Examples of puns in headlines and advertising include these:

- New Study of Obesity Looks for Larger Test Group

- Safety Experts Say School Bus Passengers Should Be Belted

- Farmer Bill Dies in House

- Hospitals are Sued by Seven Foot Doctors

- Big Rig Carrying Fruit Crashes on 210 Freeway, Creates Jam

Okay, punsters (you know who you are), carry on! As the old saying goes, "have pun, will travel."

Portmanteau Words

Lewis Carroll, author of *Alice's Adventures in Wonderland*, coined a term for words created by combining the sounds and meanings of two (or more) different words: he called it a *portmanteau* [port-MAN-toe] *word.*[54] The next time something tickles your funny bone and makes you chuckle and snort, you can thank Mr. Carroll for the descriptive word *chortle.* He also gave us *galumph* (gallop + triumph, or a triumphant gallop). I challenge you to work those words into a meaningful conversation with a loved one, teacher, or client. They will be impressed.

A portmanteau word is created when *smoke* is blended with *fog* (*=smog*), when *gigantic* is combined with *enormous* (*=ginormous*), when *information* is combined with *commercial* (*=infomercial*), when *education* is combined with *entertainment* (*=edutainment*), and when *Oxford* is combined with *Cambridge* (*=Oxbridge*).

Now that we've been enlightened by this life-changing term, *portmanteau word*, here are twenty more, used somewhere in the world every day:

- **aerobicize** (*aerobic* + *exercise*)

- **bit** (*binary* + *digit*, or *unit*)

- **blog** (*web* + *log*) (First appeared in 1999, shortly after the advent of the Worldwide Web. Not long after that, in 2002, we first see **vlog**—video + blog.)[55]

- **brunch** (*breakfast* + *lunch*)

- **cockapoo** (*cocker* [*spaniel*] + *poodle*) (Perhaps inspired by the parrot known as the *cockatoo.*)

---

[54] Linguists use the term "blend."

[55] I was surprised to learn of a much earlier use of *blog*. Roughly 100 years ago in England, *blog* was "an uncomplimentary English epithet, made up of *bloody* and *dog*." (Withington, 1925, 189)

- **docudrama** (*documentary* + *drama*)

- **electrocute** (*electric* + *execute*)

- **emoticon** (*emotion* + *icon*)

- **fantabulous** (*fantastic* + *fabulous*)

- **guesstimate** (*guess* + *estimate*)

- **happenstance** (*happen* + *circumstance*)

- **irregardless** (*irrespective* + *regardless*). Garner calls this a "semiliterate portmanteau word" that "should have been stamped out long ago."[56]

- **motel** (*motor* + *hotel*)

- **motorcade** (*motor* + *cavalcade*)

- **nylon** (*vinyl* + *rayon*)

- **simulcast** (*simultaneous* + *broadcast*)

- **slithy** (*lithe* + *slimy*)

- **tangelo** (*tangerine* + *pomelo*)

- **televangelist** (television + evangelist)

- **Vitameatavegamin** (a portmanteau word on steroids: *vitamins* + *meat* + *vegetables* + *minerals*. From *I Love Lucy*, season 1, episode thirty.)

How many of them did you know?

---

[56] Garner 2016, 529.

Mondegreens

Years ago, I read a book where the author repeatedly used the expression "beckoned call"—as in, "The clerk responded readily to his boss's every beckoned call at the office." *Beckoned call?* That was like fingernails on the chalkboard to my fussy grammar-ears. It should have been *beck and call*. And then I decided to look it up in one of my go-to language reference books: *Garner's Modern American Usage*. Not only did Garner have an entry on this quirky expression, but he also even supplied a label for slightly "off" words and expressions that result from mishearing the actual word or expression: "mondegreens."

According to Garner, a mondegreen is "a misheard lyric, saying, catchphrase, or slogan." Scottish writer Sylvia Wright introduced mondegreen to the English-speaking world in 1954 in a magazine article where she recounted how she, as a child, misunderstood a line in a popular ballad. The line was "laid him on the green," but to her young ears it was "Lady Mondegreen."

Children are good at mishearing words and song lyrics and producing clever alternatives that fit with their developing language database. Maybe you've heard of the little guy who sang "round John Virgin" instead of "round yon Virgin" in "Away in a Manger." Or the Star-Spangled Banner's "Jose can you see, by the donzerly light?" Some tykes think the letter in the alphabet between *k* and *p* is "ellemeno."

It took a while for my wife and me to figure out that Abba's song "Take a Chance on Me" featured the phrase "Honey, I'm still free," not "ollie oxen free." (True confession.)

But some mondegreens occur in adulthood, and they are often harder to shake—and more embarrassing. We say, "Little Johnny's the *spitting image* of his father," which is actually a corruption of the original *spit and image* (or *spit 'n' image*), from a time when *spit* commonly meant "perfect likeness" (you can look it up).[57]

We hear "mute point" (which should be *moot* point) and "for all intensive purposes" (make that "for all *intents and purposes*"). I heard a local television news reporter recently explain how the storm "wrecked havoc." While an understandable word choice, it's a mondegreen. The expression is *wreaked* havoc. Close, but no cigar.

The satisfying thing to me, the fellow with the sometimes fussy-grammar ears, is that I now have a label for these slightly "off" words, expressions, and sayings. Mondegreens.

---

[57] Hawking up a loogie has nothing to do with how Johnny resembles his father.

Malapropisms

A malapropism is a word that is used incorrectly—often intentionally but sometimes unintentionally—resulting in comedic effect.

"Malapropism" derives from Richard Brinsley Sheridan's 1775 play *The Rivals*, where the character Mrs. Malaprop loves big words but tends to use them incorrectly, such as, "She's as headstrong as an allegory [read *alligator*] on the banks of the Nile."

Other examples of malapropisms:

"Having but one wife (or husband) is called monotony [read *monogamy*]."

"My mother said the boogeyman in the closet was a pigment [read *figment*] of my imagination."

"Tom remembers everything perfectly because he has a photogenic [read *photographic*] memory."

"Texas has a lot of electrical [read *electoral*] votes." – attributed to Yogi Berra.

When you have an entire statement that comes out mangled, that too is a malapropism. For example,

"A verbal agreement isn't worth the paper it's written on." – attributed to Samuel Goldwyn.

"I read part of it all the way through." – attributed to Samuel Goldwyn.

Mrs. Malaprop would be proud.

Spoonerisms

One day many years ago I announced to my wife that I was going to go shake a tower. Her quizzical expression was my tipoff that I'd said something, well, a little off. Making odd, quirky comments isn't unusual for me, but it's usually intentional. Not that time. When I realized I'd said, "shake a tower" instead of "take a shower," I chuckled and mentally patted myself on the head for once again being so stinking witty. Unintentionally.

Though in my thirties, I'd never heard of Spoonerisms, which is exactly what "shake a tower" was. Garner defines a Spoonerism as "a phrase in which the initial consonants of two words are swapped, usually by accident, to create an amusing expression."[58] The Reverend W. A. Spooner, an Oxford don in the late 19th and early 20th centuries, is credited with popularizing such linguistic anomalies, like "The Lord is a shoving leopard," "It is kisstomary to cuss the bride," and, when entire words are swapped, "Work is the curse of the drinking man."[59]

A teacher at church one day said that members of a particular group "*anged in rage* from 13 to 18." He never noticed it—and, apparently, neither did anyone else—but I almost burst out laughing. I've never forgotten it. (Have you ever tried to stifle a laugh in church? It hurts.)

Author Shel Silverstein authored a book of poetry filled with Spoonersims for children, *Runny Babbit: A Billy Sook*. I haven't read it, but I'd like to.

As an adolescent living in the Bay Area in the late '60s–early '70s, I used to chuckle at the announcer's potential mangling of the Mike Tuck–Ron Fortner news program that appeared each evening on Channel 2 as the "Tuck-Fortner Report." Although what you're thinking never happened (to my

---

[58] Garner 2016, 1029.
[59] That should be, "Drink is the curse of the working man."

knowledge), it was Mike Tuck who almost stuck his foot in it when he introduced banker—and later U.S. Representative— Fortney Stark as "Fartney Stork."[60]

Serious person that I am, I occasionally pepper my conversations with Spoonerisms like the following, much to my listener's delight:

"It's a moggy forning. Be careful. It's like sea poop out there."

"Yesterday, I lent to the wake and sought a gunburn."

"I need to cake the tar to the station and gill it with fass."

"After that, I'll stow to the gore and fick up pood for dinner."

By then, my listener will be ready to mock me in the south.

Thingamajig Words

"Did you see that on Thursday they're having a careers doodad in the cafeteria?" I asked the student assistants working in my office at the college. One young lady looked up from her desk wearing a puzzled expression. I realized she might be having trouble with the odd word *doodad*. I did what we all do when we don't know or can't pull up the right word at the moment: we pluck the first generic, go-to word that comes to mind. With a moment's thought, I could have come up with something more fitting, like *event*, *affair*, *activity*, or even the universally acceptable *thing*.

I call the category of words like *doodad* "thingamajig words."[61] We all use them. Is your favorite go-to thingamajig word in the following list?

- *deely-bobber*
- *dingus*
- *dofunny*
- *doohickey*
- *doojigger*
- *doojiggy*
- flumadiddle
- *gadget*
- *gizmo*
- *hootmalalie*
- *something or other*
- *thingamabob*
- *thingamadoodle*
- *thingy*
- *whatsit*
- *what's-its-name*
- *widget*

Please safely indulge in all the thingamajigs, deely-bobbers, and doohickeys that bring joy to your life.

---

[61] I know of no one else who calls them that, but it fits and I like it.

Palindrome Fun

What's a *palindrome*, you ask? (I'm so glad you asked.) According to *Merriam-Webster's Collegiate Dictionary* (11th ed.), *palindrome* is derived from the Greek *palindromos*— "running back again" (from *palin*, back, again, and *dramein*, to run.) A palindrome is "a word, verse, or sentence (as 'Able was I ere I saw Elba') or a number (as 1881) that reads the same backward or forward." Some of you have palindrome names, like *Bob* or *Hannah*, *Otto* or *Anna*, *Mom* or *Dad*, and I salute you.

Well known palindrome sentences include these:
* *A man, a plan, a canal: Panama.*
* *A tin mug for a jar of gum, Nita.*
* *Cigar? Toss it in a can. It is so tragic.*
* *Madam, I'm Adam.*

And there is this one, the longest palindrome I've ever seen, at 47 words:

Do good? I? No! Evil anon I deliver. I maim nine more hero-men in Saginaw, sanitary sword a-tuck, Carol, I – lo! – rack, cut a drowsy rat in Aswan. I gas nine more hero-men in Miami. Reviled, I (Nona) live on. I do, O God![62]

Dates written as eight digits are sometimes the same forward and backward. They are also considered palindromes. Such eight-digit palindrome dates are exceedingly rare. In the twenty-first century there are only thirteen of them. I am writing this on the fourth palindrome day of the century (see the list below). The next one occurs on December 2, 2021, and after that, an eight-plus-year gap until the next. Here's the complete list, for your edification:

* October 2, 2001 (10022001)
* January 2, 2010 (01022010)
* November 2, 2011 (11022011)
* February 2, 2020 (02022020)
* December 2, 2021 (12022021)

---

[62] Source: http://www.rinkworks.com/words/palindromes.shtml

- March 2, 2030 (03022030)
- April 2, 2040 (04022040)
- April 2, 2040 (04022040)
- May 2, 2050 (05022050)
- June 2, 2060 (06022060)
- July 2, 2070 (07022070)
- August 2, 2080 (08022080)
- September 2, 2090 (09022090)[63]

There. Doesn't knowing this make life a little more complete? I'm sure it does.

And finally, as my dinnertime approaches, I'm reminded of this meaningful palindromic request:

Go hang a salami; I'm a lasagna hog.

---

[63] Source: https://www.livescience.com/33583-palindrome-dates-21st-century-weird.html

Avoid Cliches Like the Plague

Cliches usually weaken one's writing, and therefore we should avoid them if at all possible. A cliché is a "saying gone trite from overuse."[64] It is "something . . . that has become overly familiar or commonplace."[65]

Here are twenty examples of commonly heard clichés:

- at the end of the day
- blissful ignorance
- comparing apples and oranges
- conspicuous by its absence
- far be it from me
- few and far between
- first and foremost
- high and dry
- hit the nail on the head
- it's a no-brainer
- mental toughness
- moment of truth
- my better half
- nip it in the bud (with apologies to Barney Fife fans)
- on the same page
- six of one, half a dozen of the other
- throw the baby out with the bath water
- viable alternative
- with that being said (or *having said that*, or *that said*)
- yada, yada, yada

One can't always avoid using a cliché (plague or not), but we should try to use them sparingly.

---

[64] Garner 2016, 173.
[65] Merriam-Webster 2020.

Twelve Latin-based (or Latinate)[66] expressions useful to know

As you are no doubt aware, English is a polyglot fed by many linguistic tributaries, including Latin.

A reasonably well-educated writer of English should feel confident to employ these useful and relatively common terms and phrases borrowed directly from Latin.

- **ad hoc** – lit. "for this." Often used for specific or immediate problems or needs. (E.g., "The college president appointed an ad hoc committee to study ways to improve student graduation rates.")

- **ad hominem** – lit. "to the person." An attack on a person's character or motives rather than the policy or position that they maintain.

- **caveat emptor** – lit. "let the buyer beware."

- **de facto** – lit. "in fact, or in effect." (E.g., "The state is de facto divided into two states.")

- **ex nihilo** – lit. "from or out of nothing." (E.g., "Christian doctrine teaches that God created the universe ex nihilo.")

- **ipso facto** – lit. "by the fact itself; by its very nature."

- **non sequitur** – lit. "it does not follow." A conclusion or statement that does not logically follow from the previous argument or statement."

- **persona non grata** – lit. "an unacceptable person."

- **post hoc ergo propter hoc** – lit. "after this, therefore because of this." (often shortened to *post hoc*). The logical fallacy that attributes the cause of an event or condition to something unrelated that

---

[66] Latinate – "An adjective: of, relating to, resembling, or derived from Latin."

happened before it. (E.g., a rooster crows, the sun rises; therefore, the rooster's crow causes the sun to rise.)

- **quid pro quo** – lit. "something for something." Something given or received for something else.

- **sic** – lit. "so, thus." Intentionally so written; used after a printed word or passage to indicate that it is intended exactly as printed. It is enclosed in brackets immediately after the word or words referred to. (E.g., "Mr. Jones reported, 'I seen [*sic*] the man running across the street.")

- **status quo** – lit. "the state in which." The existing state of affairs.

Also see "Commonly Used (and Misused) Latinate Abbreviations" above.

Twelve French-based expressions useful to know

A reasonably well-educated writer of English should feel confident to employ these useful and relatively common terms and phrases borrowed directly from French.[67]

- **bon appetit** – lit. "good appetite." (Pronounced bone apuh-TEE.) Its general meaning is "enjoy your meal" or "happy eating."

- **bon vivant** – lit. "good liver" (i.e., one who lives well). A bon vivant is someone with refined tastes—especially with regard to food and drink.

- **bon voyage** – lit. "good journey." It typically means "Farewell!" or "Have a good trip!"

- **faux pas** – lit. "false step." A faux pas is a social blunder.

- **faux-naïf** – lit. "falsely naïve." It usually refers to someone or something that is falsely childlike or simple. (E.g., "Harpo Marx always played a faux-naïf role in the Marx Brothers movies.")

- **haute couture** – lit. "high sewing" or "high dressmaking." Refers to high-fashion clothing or the houses or designers who create trend-setting fashions for women.

- **haute cuisine** – lit. "high cooking." Artful or elaborate cuisine.

- **joie de vivre** – lit. "joy of living." A keen or buoyant enjoyment of life. (E.g., "The woman's spontaneous dance showed her joie de vivre."

---

[67] The following information is taken or adapted from *Merriam-Webster's College Dictionary*, 11th edition and *New Oxford American Dictionary*, 3rd edition.

- **laissez faire** – lit. "to let (people) do as they please." (E.g., "The government exhibited a laissez faire approach to mending the ailing economy.")

- **nom de plume** – lit. "pen name." (E.g., "Samuel Clemens's nom de plume was Mark Twain.")

- **raison d'être** – lit. "reason or justification for existence." (E.g., "Composing beautiful music was Mozart's raison d'être.")

- **tête-à-tête** – lit. "head-to-head." A private conversation between two persons.

Of Cranks, Bugs, and Fans[68]

When the United States began to recover from the terrible trauma of the Civil War in the 1860s, '70s, and '80s, the game of baseball provided a healing tonic for many Americans. Baseball (or *base ball*, as it was typically spelled) had been  around in one form or another for several decades prior to the Civil War, but it was that national tragedy that provided fertile soil for the sport to grow exponentially in popularity. Soldiers from both Northern and Southern armies played baseball, and they took it home with them when their military service ended. A mere four years after Lee's surrender at Appomattox, the first professional baseball team had formed in Cincinnati, and two years after that, in 1871, the first professional baseball league had been (loosely) organized.

Cranks

As baseball's popularity skyrocketed, newspapers featured detailed accounts of games, box scores reduced each contest to a quick-and-easy statistical snapshot, and top ball players—or "ballists"—became the idols of boys everywhere (men, too, if they were honest). Enthusiastic devotees rose up from all walks of life, but guardians of polite society frowned upon them and referred to them as "cranks," a decidedly pejorative term. A crank was someone who wasn't quite right in the head—bent, crooked, out-of-joint mentally, overly enthusiastic about a subject or activity. He was considered uncultured and unruly—not somebody you'd want your daughter to socialize with at the church picnic.

Fans

By the late 1880s, the national game needed a new term for its devoted followers, and we began to see "rooter" occasionally

---

[68] Dean Christensen, *Nothing About Baseball Is Trivial: Essential Terms, Rules, Stats & History for Fans and Wannabe Fans* (Monee, IL: Independently Published, 2021), 17, 21-22, 23-24.

and "fan"—short for fanatic—appearing in newspapers and magazines. *Fanatic*—from the Latin *fanaticus*: "mad, frantic, enthusiastic, inspired by deity," a word with roots in *fanum*, "temple"—wasn't initially much of an improvement over *crank* in its derogatory connotations. But when Cincinnati sportswriter Ren Mulford Jr. popularized the abbreviated form, *fan*, it caught on. As the national game evolved into the National Pastime, *crank* and *rooter* fell by the wayside and *fan* took its place in America's sports lexicon. Soon it lost its less than complimentary connotation, and baseball devotees everywhere proudly wore the *fan* moniker.

Bugs

But we're not done with this story. Early in the twentieth century another word came on the scene, featured in Tin Pany Alley songs of the era: *bug*. This term for a baseball fan, popular between roughly 1904 and 1916, was borrowed from the everyday slang for an unspecified illness, which we still use today: "I came down with a bug and was sick for a week." In the early twentieth century, baseball devotees might say they were stricken with baseball fever—that they had "caught the baseball bug." It didn't take long for that "sickness" to be applied to the person himself or herself: one didn't simply *catch* the bug; one *was* a bug—a baseball bug.

But *bug* didn't have the staying power of *fan*, and by 1920, *fan* had regained its dominant place in the American baseball lexicon. Soon, all sports had their fans. It's true that some fans today are *fanatical*, in the earlier sense of the word: borderline crazy, frantic, and seemingly possessed by a deity that exists in the form of their favorite team or sport. We call them *rabid* fans—another term borrowed from the realm of disease—or "dyed-in-the-wool" fans. But I suspect that most fans nowadays would say they are knowledgeable about their sport, that they enjoy watching or playing it, that they follow the achievements of their favorite teams and players, and that they simply enjoy the camaraderie of like-minded folks.

Baseball fans in California share something special with baseball fans in Texas, and Missouri, and Illinois, and New York. Though our cultures may differ, we share a common interest and heritage as fans. And American fans share those same things with fans in Mexico, the Dominican Republic, Puerto Rico, Japan, Korea, and many other places throughout the world. That commonality of interest unites us in ways few other things do. And that's why I'm proud to say I'm a baseball fan.

But when I want to be quirky—which is frequently—I just say

... I'm a bug.

How I Might Know If You're From England

You *might* be from England (or the UK) if ...

. . . you usually tag an *–s* onto the word *toward*. The preferred British spelling is *towards*. The preferred American spelling is simply *toward* (no *–s*). When I copyedit a document written for American readers, almost the first thing I do is to execute a global search-and-replace to eliminate all those pesky *s*'s (if there are any) in one automated swoop. A copyediting instructor years ago taught me that trick. (Shhh! . . . let's keep it our little secret.)

. . . you often use single quotation marks for quoted words and sentences instead of double quotation marks. 'You guessed it, good fellow. I'm from Liverpool', (British)

instead of, "You guessed it, good fellow. I'm from Denver," (American). In American English, we use single quotation marks for quotes *within* quotes, such as, "Here's the answer he gave," said the investigator. "He said, 'I'm from Denver.'" Otherwise, we use double quotation marks for quoted words and sentences. To make it ridiculously complicated, in British English that punctuation scheme is reversed. What were they thinking? Next thing you know they'll be driving on the wrong side of the road too.

. . . you tend to place your commas and periods *outside* of quotation marks* instead of *inside* them. Here's an example: *The film critic from the* Times *wrote that the latest sequel was "pabulum not befitting an infant", but the critic from the* Daily News *countered that it was "a feast fit for a king".* Note the placement of the comma and period there. In the US we would keep that comma and period tucked safely inside (to the left of) the quotation marks. And that's true even if just one word is enclosed in quotation marks. Try it, you'll like it!

So there you go: a simple, non-exhaustive test for determining if in fact you might have grown up in England, or some other land where British English is used, and had somehow forgotten that fact.[69]**

---

[69] With apologies to my friends across the pond for this tongue-in-cheek piece. It wasn't my intent to be cheeky. If this essay seems like tosh, I may be a nit, but hopefully not an oik.

Clippings – How to spell words we often abbreviate when spoken

Speakers of English tend to shorten or truncate longer words, both in writing and speaking. That's the way we are; it's normal. I call such truncated words *clippings*. Sometimes we drop the initial syllable or syllables. Examples are *airplane* → *plane*; *hamburger* → *burger*; and *telephone* → *phone*.[70] When we drop the ending syllable or syllables, examples include *popular* → *pop*; *public* → *pub*; and *technician* → *tech*.[71] Occasionally, we have both the beginning and the ending of the word dropped, leaving us with *influenza* → *flu*; and *refrigerator* → *frig*. Wait. *Frig*? Get me a cold one from the *frig*? Hmmm. More on that one below.

When it comes to writing such clipped words, how do we spell them? Here's the **principle**: We generally spell a clipped word as it *sounds,* not necessarily as a sliced off version of the original. Following are some common examples, with the original word followed by the shortened form.

Favorite—*fave*. "Rocky road ice cream is my fave" (not *fav*, which, the way I hear it in my head, rhymes with *fab*). Remember: we spell clipped forms as they *sound*.

Microphone—*mike*. "Please turn on the mike" (not the *mic*). When I read *mic* for microphone, I hear "mick." Now, I understand it's tempting and easy to write *mic*, but consider this argument against that spelling: What do we do when *mic* is used as a verb and written in past tense or as a present participle? "The sound tech *miced* the singer"? (That conjures up some interesting images.) Or "We will be *micing* all candidates on this evening's debate panel." (And after that I suppose we'll be slicing and dicing them?) Let's solve that and spell it *mike*.

---

[70] I'm grateful for Bryan A. Garner's informing me in his outstanding book *The Chicago Guide to Grammar, Usage, and Punctuation* that there is a word for this type of clipped word: aphaeresis (ə-**fer**-ə-səs). My life is now complete.
[71] This sort of clipped form is called an apocope (ə-**pok**- ə-pee). (Thank you again, Mr. Garner.)

Refrigerator—*fridge*. "The potato salad is in the fridge" (not the *frig*). When I see *frig* I hear a word in my head that rhymes with *brig* (where they lock up misbehavers in the military) or *trig* (short for trigonometry). The refrigerator ain't a friggin' *frig*. It's a *fridge*, dadgummit!

Here's another fun fact about *frig*. (Shhhh . . . I'm whispering now so any nearby children can't hear). According to my fave everyday dictionary, *Merriam-Webster's Collegiate*, *frig* is a verb that comes from the Middle English *fryggen*, to wiggle, and is "often vulgar: copulate—sometimes used in the present participle as a meaningless intensive" (as, for example, in my sentence above—"The refrigerator ain't a friggin' frig").

So let's please keep our fridges and our frigs separate. Hand me a mike and I'll make that announcement.

Clippings – Part 2

"Clipped" words are words that are commonly shortened. It's easy to see how many multi-syllable words came to be abbreviated, because that's the nature of informal communications.

For example, we obviously get *phone* from *telephone*, *photo* from *photograph*, and *bio* from *biography*—all easy to understand and simple to spell.

In some instances, the spelling of a clipped form changes based on how the word is pronounced, how it *sounds* to the ear. So for example (to review), the clipped form of

- *refrigerator* is spelled *fridge* (not *frig*);
- *favorite* becomes *fave* (not *fav*);
- *microphone* is shortened to *mike* (not *mic*).

Additionally,

- *cousin* becomes *cuz* (not *cous*; in my head I hear either *couscous*—pronounced *coose-coose*—as in the African dish of steamed semolina, or *couse* [rhyming with *house*];

* and *bicycle* and *tricycle* become *bike* and *trike* (not *bic* and *tric*—although we do alter them a bit to end with a hard -*k* sound).

We often don't realize how many common, everyday words are actually abbreviated forms of multi-syllable words. So are you up for a little quiz? Do you know the full word from which we get the following twelve clipped forms? Some have been part of the English vernacular for 150–200 years. (I can assure you, I didn't know a few of these myself.)

See the footnote below for the answers.

1. bus
2. cello
3. fan (as in *baseball fan*)
4. pants
5. prep
6. pub
7. quad (as in the enclosed outdoor square typically found on a school campus)
8. quotes
9. specs
10. taxi
11. typo
12. zoo[72]

Well, how did you do? A long time ago, linguists, lexicographers (people who compile dictionaries for a living), and English teachers frowned on the use of any abbreviated forms, but the practice is widely accepted today. As in the case of all word choices, for the purpose of effective communication, clarity is the number one rule. It's best to

---

[72]Answers: 1. omnibus; 2. violoncello; 3. fanatic; 4. pantaloons; 5. prepare or preparatory; 6. public house; 7. quadrangle; 8. quotation marks or quotations; 9. spectacles (i.e., eyeglasses) or specifications; 10. taximeter cab; 11. typographer or typographical error; 12. zoological garden.
Sources: R. W. Burchfield's *The New Fowler's Modern English Usage*, 3rd edition; *Merriam-Webster's Collegiate Dictionary.*

spell out any word that our readers might not readily understand.

Omnibus

Violoncello (Yes, it's spelled correctly.)

How to Write "God" Words

When I write a word with "God" in it, I sometimes need to pause to make sure I'm capitalizing—or not capitalizing—the word appropriately. Given my lifelong Christian faith, my first thought is to capitalize almost all such words. If "God" is in it, out of reverence, the word should be capitalized. But is that necessary or grammatically correct?

The truth is, most "God" words are actually "god" words, with lowercase g's, and writing them according to long-established and widely accepted conventions of Standard Written English does not make a person of faith less faithful. Let's consider the most common "God" words.[73]

A small handful of words with "God" should normally be capitalized. We are essentially talking about three words here: (1) **God** (of course) as the designation for the supreme being acknowledged by monotheistic faiths as the creator and ruler of the universe; (2) **Godspeed,** from the Middle English *God spede you,* meaning "God prosper you" or "may God give you success" (on your journey); and (3) **God's acre,** an old word of Germanic origin meaning the churchyard or burial ground. And that, folks, is about it.

The following "god" words, however, all begin with a lowercase *g,* according to most widely accepted conventions:

- *god* (for a divine or supernatural being other than the God of monotheistic religions, or for a person or thing of supreme value)

- *god-awful* (abominable, disagreeable—note the hyphen there)

- *goddamn* (or *goddamned* or *goddam*)

---

[73] I've consulted several sources for this, including *Merriam-Webster's Collegiate Dictionary,* 11th ed., and *The Christian Writer's Manual of Style.*

- *goddess* (a female god, or a woman of great beauty or charm)

- *godfather; godmother; godson; goddaughter; godchild; godparent*

- *godforsaken* (remote, desolate, neglected, miserable)

- *godhead* (the divine nature of God, especially as existing in three persons [i.e., the Trinity or triune God])

- *godhood* (the quality or state of being a god; divinity)

- *godless* (not acknowledging a deity or divine law)

- *godlike* (resembling or having the qualities of God or a god)

- *godling* (a minor god)

- *godly* (divine; pious, devout)

- *godsend* (something desirable or needed that comes unexpectedly)

So we find that, according to Standard Written English, only three "God" words begin with capital *g*: *God* and the now nearly extinct *Godspeed* and *God's acre*. All the rest begin with a lowercase *g*.

Spelling Problem: To Double or Not to Double?

Is it *benefited* or *benefitted*? *Totaled* or *totalled*? Here's an uncomplicated way to know.

Have you ever handwritten a note and wondered if the past tense of a verb like *total* should have one *l* (tota*led*) or two (tota*lled*)? Or if the verb *benefit* should have one *t* (benefi*ted*) or two (benefi*tted*)? I consider myself a good speller, but words like that have always given me pause, and I will often consult a dictionary to check myself. However, a dictionary isn't always handy—and even using an app on my phone eats up precious time if I'm in a hurry. Isn't there a simple spelling rule to memorize that covers situations like these?

When to Double the Final Consonant

I'm glad you asked! Normally, you merely add –*ed* to a regular verb in the past tense and the past participle,[74] but regular verbs that end in consonants like *l, p, s,* or *t* can be tricky. Remember this spelling rule for doubling the final consonant:

A final consonant that is immediately preceded by an accented short vowel[75] is doubled before the –*ed* ending.

For example, *stop→stopped* (the final consonant, *p,* is immediately preceded by the accented short vowel *o,* and therefore is doubled); *bat* (the verb)→*batted* (the *t* is preceded by the accented short *a,* and therefore is doubled); You get the picture.

---

[74] To review: regular verbs do not change form—the base word remains the same: e.g., *charge, charged, charged; drop, dropped, dropped; love, loved, loved.* Irregular verbs are another story. Remember, an irregular verb changes form in its past tense or past participle. E.g., *give, gave, given; stink, stank, stunk; do, did, done; win, won, won.*
[75] When a vowel is accented, it is stressed or emphasized.

When *Not* to Double the Final Consonant

If you've grasped the above paragraph, this surely won't shock you:

If the final consonant of the verb is *not* immediately preceded by an accented short vowel, do *not* double the consonant.

For example, *total→totaled* (the *l* is not immediately preceded by an accented short vowel—the a is not stressed—so do not double it); *benefit→benefited* (again, the final consonant *t* is not preceded by an accented short vowel, so do not double it). Got it? Good![76]

Oh, and this works for present participles (verbs ending in *−ing*) as well. So we have *stopping, batting,* and *rebelling,* and we have *totaling* and *benefiting.* Fun? You betcha!

I hope that memorizing this simple spelling rule for when to double or not to double will instantly make you a better speller. If not, I guarantee double your money back.[77]

---

[76] I'm indebted to George O. Curme's *A Grammar of the English Language—Volume I: Parts of Speech* (1935) for its clear, concise explanation of this spelling rule. Keep in mind that when I refer to the "accented" short vowel, I'm referring to the syllable that is stressed.

[77] Of course, I'm joking here (in case I have to clarify that).

The "Wright" Stuff

Words and word origins have always fascinated me. My next book may very well be devoted entirely to etymology. But for now, I'd like to share a few interesting ones . . . such as the word *wright* and a few common compound words derived from *wright*.

A *wright* is "a worker skilled in the manufacture especially of wooden objects." From the Old English *wyrhta* – a worker, maker.

Cartwright – A proper name (only). Think actresses Angela and Veronica, or *Bonanza's* Ben, Little Joe, and Hoss. One might think a cartwright is one who makes or repairs carts. But nope, that would be the *wainwright* (see below).

Playwright – One who writes plays. (Be careful with the spelling on this one. It's tempting to write *playwrite*, but that would be an error.

Shipwright – A carpenter skilled in ship construction and repair.

Wainwright – A maker and repairer of wagons.

Wheelwright – A maker and repairer of wheels and wheeled vehicles.

A Caveat

Be careful not to muck up the spelling of *copyright*, which focuses on the legal *right* of copy (printed matter), not the *making* of copy (therefore not *copywright*), nor the *writing* of copy (therefore *copywrite*—although, to confuse you really good: there is such a thing as a copywriter, one who writes copy. That sort of "copywrite" is not the same as "copyright." Got it? I thought so.)

111

Should It Be *Pleaded* or *Pled*?

Watching a news program recently on PBS, I heard two different narrators give two different past tense renderings of the legal term "plead"—as in "What do you plead to these charges?" A female reporter said the congressman "pleaded" not guilty. In an unrelated story a male reporter said a defendant "pled" not guilty. Why the different words? Which is the preferred usage?

I don't recall the nationality of the two reporters, but I do know that speakers of British English consider *plead* to be a regular verb and therefore will use the regular past tense, *pleaded*.[78] In American English, the irregular verb form *pled* is considered to be an informal but acceptable usage.

The call is yours to make. If I were writing a formal essay or letter, I would use the almost universally accepted standard form *pleaded*.

---

[78] As you will recall, a verb is "regular" when its past or past participle is formed by adding -*d* or -*ed*. Most verbs are regular.

Chapter 6
A Dean's English Potpourri

In my blog, *The Dean's English*, I've written on several topics that are not specifically usage, punctuation, grammar, word-related subjects. Nonetheless, I would like to include some of those essays, which I'll call a Dean's English potpourri.[79]

Short and Sweet Communications Are Usually Best

What is your typical communication style?

Effective communication is a major challenge for most of us. I'm not talking about simple willingness to speak or write, nor merely to be a good listener,[80] both of which are important aspects of effective communication. As for being willing to speak, we all know people who can talk our ears off—usually about themselves—no matter what the original topic was, at the slightest provocation. They seem neither to notice nor care if we're tracking with them. There's a word for this clueless babbling: **logorrhea** (law-ga-REE-a).[81] Informally, I call it the *yada-yadas* or the *blah-blah-blahs*. But logorrhea is descriptive and has a certain ick factor because of the *–rrhea*

---

[79] Since I am author, editor, and publisher, I humbly exercise my privilege to include whatever I want in these pages. My readers are free to read all, some, or none of this chapter. For maximum benefit, however, I humbly encourage them to read all. (Are you catching my extreme humility here?)

[80] Listening is incredibly important. I recently watched a movie where one of the principal characters said these simple yet profound words: "Listening is loving."

[81] Etymologically, *logorrhea* means "flowing words." *Merriam-Webster Collegiate Dictionary* 11th ed. defines *logorrhea* as "excessive and often incoherent talkativeness or wordiness."

suffix it shares with another well-known word. I don't know of anybody yet who's called in sick to work because they were up all night with a bad case of logorrhea, but it could happen.

Some folks aren't necessarily afflicted with logorrhea but still talk (or write) too much. Their tendency is to **overexplain** simple concepts, using fifty words where five or ten would suffice. Overexplainers either assume you are too dense to understand what they're saying, or they don't fully understand it themselves, so by filling the ether, or the email, or the text message, with words, words, and more words they hope to sort it out in their own minds. How does it feel to be the recipient of an overexplainer's overexplanation? For me, it sometimes feels like I'm being **patronized**. To patronize someone is to treat them in a condescending way. No Bueno.

Active listening is a key to effective interpersonal communication. Some people are good at listening—at least seemingly so. They are able to tune in to the speaker, stay focused, and give periodic signals that they're tracking with the speaker such as "Uh-huh," "You got that right," "Oh, boy!" and "Tell me more about it," and nonverbals like head nods, smiles, creased brows, looks of surprise, and other appropriate facial expressions. I've always been a fairly decent listener—definitely not a *yada-yada* type of person—so I'm easy prey for the speaker afflicted with logorrhea. Fair warning: if you're going to say to someone "Tell me more about that" (presuming you're able to sneak a word in edgewise), you're asking for more *yada-yada* and *blah-blah-blah*—you have no one to blame but yourself.

Lastly, there is the person who speaks (or writes) way too little.[82] I wrote an email once to a person about a small copyediting project I had completed for them. I said something to the effect of, "Here is what I've done . . . now, I want to be sure you received my other two completed projects. Please confirm." The person's reply? "Thank you." That's it.

---

[82] Yes, of course there are more communication styles than these four—for another essay in another book.

Just "thank you." Apparently, they stopped reading after "here's what I've done" and figured that the rest of my message was just *blah-blah-blah*. D'oh!

Then there was the text message I sent to a different person a while back briefly explaining an important situation regarding a mutual acquaintance. I not only gave information but I also *sought* information, asking a question. I carefully edited my text to weed out the *yada-yadas* as much as possible but still typed a message with full (and grammatically correct) sentences. My correspondent answered with a four-word reply, which did not answer my question. So I formulated a second text and got back a one-word reply, still not answering the question. I began to wonder if it was my fault. Was I operating under the illusion that my message was clear? I sent a third message—again using complete sentences—and received a three-word non-answer reply. Bottom line: my correspondent wrote a *grand total* of eight words without addressing my question. So I gave up. Words to describe this person's type of (non)communication style are ***terse***, ***curt***, ***brusque***, and ***laconic***. Some would say ***rude*** or ***dismissive***. I realize that sometimes people are terribly busy or distracted or important and can't always take the time to formulate thoughtful replies. But come on!

If we're going to communicate effectively, we can strive to be brief, pleasant, and to the point, using full sentences and correct grammar (especially in writing—yes, *even text messages*. Gasp!). We keep logorrhea to a minimum, we don't patronize, we listen (or read) actively, and we avoid terse, dismissive messages. There's an expression for this type of thoughtful communication style: ***short and sweet***. That's what I aim for—most of the time, anyway.

Poetic License? But Why?

Standard English took a blow below the belt with the rise of rock 'n' roll music, and it was only a matter of time before the assault on the mother tongue would be sanctified by Christian artists writing "Jesus Music," beginning in the '70s.

 I was no grammar snob as a teenager and young adult, but neither was I a grammar slob. I lived for the rock 'n' roll music of Randy Stonehill, Daniel Amos, and other pioneers of the Christian rock genre. I slapped on my Pioneer stereo headphones, cranked up the volume, and blew out my eardrums on a regular basis to songs like

He's the rock that doesn't roll, He's the rock that doesn't roll; He's good for the body and great for the soul—he's the rock that doesn't roll.[83]

If you loved that classic by the "Father of Christian Rock," Larry Norman, give me a hearty "right on!" I played the vinyl LP until the grooves had worn down and then recorded it on my cassette player and listened to the tape until it had stretched out of shape.[84] It wasn't deep theology. But at least it was grammatically correct, which can't be said of all Jesus Music of that era.

And then I grew up—an assertion my wife and grown children might not corroborate. After all these years, what sometimes passes for songwriting in contemporary Christian circles leaves me scratching my head—both from a musical standpoint and from a grammatical point of view.[85] The latter is the focus of this essay.

---

[83] Larry Norman, from his *In Another Land* album, circa 1976.
[84] Not really. I'm using hyperbole to make a point.

[85] By "musical standpoint" I'm referring to a song's singability in a congregational setting—a topic I could write multiple pages on because so much contemporary Christian music that is popular on the radio is simply not singable in the context of congregational worship. But the emphasis of this post is on lyrics, not music.

A recent popular song features the recurring lyric,

The same power that rose Jesus from the grave . . .

When I first heard that, it was fingernails scraping the chalkboard—an egregious affront to my grammatical sensibilities. Why? Why would an ostensibly literate songwriter use *rose* when he should have used *raised*? We're not talking a different *form* of the same verb—we're talking two different *verbs*. Yes, they are related, but they are different verbs.

Here's a twenty-five-cent tutorial on the difference between the two:

Rose is the past tense of the verb **rise**, which is intransitive. An intransitive verb has no direct object—the subject performs the action by itself/himself/herself.

- "The sun *[subject]* rose *[verb]*."
- "The spectators *[subject]* rose *[verb]* when the judge walked into the courtroom."

Raised is the past tense of the verb **raise**, which is transitive. A transitive verb has a direct object—the subject performs an action on something.

- "The flag monitor *[subject]* raised *[verb]* the American flag *[direct object]* each morning."
- "The farmer *[subject]* raised *[verb]* a crop of corn *[direct object]*"
- "The same power *[subject]* that raised *[verb]* Jesus *[direct object]* from the grave . . ."

How would it sound if we said, "The flag monitor rose the American flag," or "The farmer rose his corn crop"? It might be jes' fine if we was tryin' out fer Jed Clampett in *The Return of the Beverly Hillbillies*; otherwise not so much.

In the song in question, the songwriter chose the incorrect verb. Even considering the possibility that he intentionally selected *rose* instead of *raised* in the name of poetic license, I can only ask, *Why*, for Pete's sake? My friend who drew this convoluted bit of song lyric to my attention pointed out that *raised* is closer in sound to *grave* than *rose* is. So for the sake of poetry alone, the writer should have used the correct verb: *The same power that **raised** Jesus from the **grave** . . .*

Okay, in case I've alienated half my readers at this point, to you I say, "I'm sorry." If that song is meaningful in your life—wonderful! May God bless you for it. And if I get to heaven and find out it was one of God's favorites—oopsie! He may have to give me a timeout on a stool in the corner for a couple of thousand years.

But for now, for me, it's only scrape, scratch, scritch on the chalkboard of my mind.[86]

---

[86] Okay, don't I sound like a curmudgeon here? About some things, I definitely am.

Acronyms and Initialisms

My colleagues in education often joked that our realm was all about acronyms. I used to laugh at that until I sat down one day and tried to list all the acronyms for departments and programs used on our campus. Writer's cramp forced me to stop before I'd gotten halfway through. But the joke was on me when I discovered that there are *acronyms* and there are *initialisms* and, although similar, they are technically not the same. We all must love acronyms and initialisms as we use them all the time.

Acronyms

Acronyms are abbreviations of multi-word nouns, consisting of the initial letters of each word and are *pronounceable* words. That last phrase is key. For example, the National Aeronautics and Space Administration is universally known by its acronym *NASA*, and "Light Amplification by Stimulated Emission of Radiation" is the mouthful better known by the acronym *laser.*

The acronym, like its cousin the initialism, is generally written all in caps with no periods, unless it's a word like *laser,* or *scuba*, or *snafu*. (Don't look up that last one unless you're over eighteen.) Remember the "no periods" part. I still kick myself for missing S.T.E.M. (Science, Technology, Engineering, and Math) in a document I copyedited for a PR specialist a few years ago.[87]

Initialisms

If the abbreviation is not pronounceable as a word, it's an initialism.[88] We pronounce each letter individually. The

---

[87] I debated with myself about leaving the periods in and finally decided to do so—but further research revealed I should have suggested *STEM*, without the periods. Trivial things like that keep copyeditors awake at night.

[88] Also called an *alphabetism*.

familiar combinations *FBI*, *CIA*, and *IBM* are initialisms and not, strictly speaking, acronyms.

So I discovered that the majority of abbreviated departments and programs on my campus were actually *initialisms*, such as *EOPS* (Extended Opportunity Programs and Services, not to be confused with *EOP*—Educational Opportunity Program), *DSPS* (Disabled Students Programs and Services), and *CGE* (Continuing and Global Education). I was always tempted to be cagey and make that one a true acronym (*CAGE*) because of the *and* in there, but it wasn't appreciated. This discovery of the difference between acronyms and initialisms was, to me, an almost life-changing revelation.

Usage Tips

Here are four tips for writing acronyms and initialisms:

1. Go easy with them, especially if you write for a technical or scientific field. A document is clunky when filled with too many abbreviations, and people won't want to read it.

2. In formal writing it's best to write out the acronym or initialism on its first occurrence *if* it's likely to be unfamiliar to some readers. So I might write out "Food and Drug Administration" the first time and then in subsequent references use its initialism, *FDA*. If it's a well-known abbreviation, there's probably no need to spell it out. *NASA* is a good example, or *JPEG*, which is an interesting combination of initialism (*J*) and acronym (*PEG*).[89]

3. It's important to know which indefinite article should precede an acronym or initialism—whether *a* or *an*. Referring to a medical doctor, should it be "*a* MD" or "*an* MD"? It's decided by how the abbreviation is pronounced, whether with an opening consonant or vowel sound. "MD" is pronounced "em-dee," an opening vowel sound, so the correct article to use is *an*: "*an* MD." A Doctor of Veterinary Medicine,

---

[89] To make it simple, I'll just call *JPEG* an acronym if you don't mind. Thanks.

however, would be "*a* DVM" because the initialism begins with a consonant.

4. Periods are rarely needed with these things today. So it's *DNA, CGI, IRS, HMO, VFW,* and *USA.* Even two-letter abbreviations need no periods, like *BA, MA, MD,* or *US,* all of which routinely appeared with periods in the past (*B.A., U.S.,* etc.). One caveat: if the organization you're writing about uses periods in their own acronym, then you should, too. You don't want to irritate your teacher or client.

Making Better Lists

Often the best way to convey a lot of information with maximum clarity in minimum space is through vertical lists. Vertical lists work well for brochures, flyers, and reports; website content; PowerPoint presentations; and resumes and cover letters. Done well, vertical lists will help your readers quickly and easily comprehend the vital information you want them to know.

But "done well" is easier said than done, and constructing vertical lists that are clear, concise, and consistent can be tricky. So here are some tips for avoiding common list-making errors and for creating bang-up vertical lists that will add zip and polish to your next project.

The first principle to keep in mind is *parallel structure*, and the key to parallel structure is *consistency*. Parallel structure includes (among other things) organizing the list so that each item begins in a comparable manner. For example, if you're talking about actions, try to begin *every list item* with an action word (i.e., a verb), and typically you should make sure items are either all single words or short phrases *or* all complete sentences. In the following example, the elements are parallel—each item is a phrase (not a complete sentence) and each begins with a verb.

> *Here's what our team of auto-care specialists will do when you bring in your car or truck:*

- Change the oil and filter
- Check the tire pressure
- Top off all fluids
- Inspect the brakes
- Rotate the tires (as needed)
- Replace non-working blinker bulbs

Often, however, we'll see a list formatted with little regard for parallel structure, such as this one:

> *Here's what our team of auto-care specialists will do when you bring in your car or truck:*

- Change the oil and filter
- Tire pressure
- Fluids
- Thorough brake inspection
- If needed, rotate the tires
- We'll even replace your non-working blinker bulbs

Did you notice how the first item in the list began with a verb, the second with a noun, the third with just a single word (a noun), the fourth with an adjective, the fifth with a conditional phrase, and the sixth item was a complete sentence. That's kind of crazy, but it's how many people format their vertical lists.

When the elements are parallel, it's easier for your reader to quickly comprehend the information.

The second principle for making great lists is to be consistent with formatting. Lists should generally be introduced with a complete sentence followed by a colon. For example,

Here are the ingredients for a delicious pineapple upside-down cake:

If the listed items are complete sentences, they should be punctuated as complete sentences, including ending each item with a period. If they are single words or short phrases, no ending punctuation is required (as in the lists above). If, however, the list items complete the introductory element, each should be ended with a semicolon, as in the following:

The skills and qualifications that set me apart from the rest include

- top-notch computer literacy;
- outstanding customer service;
- a strong commitment to diversity; and
- excellent communication skills.

Notice how there was no punctuation after the introductory element because the list items complete the sentence—in vertical form. Each item is separated from the following one by a semicolon (not a comma), and the final item terminates the list-sentence with a period. (The *and* before the last item is optional.) You will also notice that each item is a particular skill or ability preceded by an adjective.

Here's a final word on using bullets, numbers, or nothing at all before items. There is no hard-and-fast rule on this, but you should heed a couple of principles:

The Principle of Logic. If you are creating a list of steps in a process, chapters in a book, or something that needs to have some logical sequence or ordering, it's usually best to use numbers instead of bullets. If no particular order is needed, perhaps arranging the items alphabetically would make logical sense.

The Principle of Consistency. When using bullets, try to use the same or similar bullets throughout. Bold, black dots (like those used in the examples above) are often best. Or you might choose to use square bullets or horizontal dashes. Whatever you use, try to keep all bullets in the document or page the same. I've seen job seekers "dress up" their resumes with fancy wingding bullets: stars, pointing fingers, balloons, pretty flowers, and the like. Unless you're making a flyer for a party or another lighthearted purpose, stick to simple bullets—or even none at all.

A well-organized and styled vertical list will maximize limited space, help your readers quickly grasp the information, and impress those readers with your solid grasp of Standard Written English. As a result, you will better serve your customers and clients, and maybe even gain an edge on your competition.

"Favorite" Grammar and Usage Pet Peeves

It's always fun to share our grammar and usage pet peeves, isn't it? (Please, just humor me and nod your head. Thanks.) Here, then, are just a few of my "favorite" grammar, punctuation, and usage pet peeves, in no particular order.[90]

Using apostrophes to make words plural.

As in "We are open Friday's from 10 a.m. to 6 p.m." Or "I received lot's of presents for Christmas." No. Apostrophe-*s* doesn't make a word plural. In both of these examples, just add an *s*. Please don't commit Apostrophe Abuse.

Randomly capitalizing words in a sentence.

As in the sentence immediately above.

Here's another example: "Yesterday, my Mom went to the Doctor for her annual Checkup, and then went to the Grocery Store." Nope. None of those words except Yesterday should be capitalized. Proper nouns (names and titles) should be capitalized, but in this sentence, doctor is neither. It's a common noun, and common nouns aren't capitalized. Same thing for mom. In our example, mom is not a name, it's a common noun, just as brother, sister, cousin, friend, or neighbor are common nouns. If I had left out the pronoun my and written, "Yesterday, Mom went to the doctor . . .," then it should be capitalized. Why? Because I'm using Mom as a name, which makes it a proper noun, which means it should be capitalized.

Writing (or saying) "based *off*" of something.

I'm not sure how this got introduced to the vernacular, but its use is widespread. Let's get the preposition right: it should be that something is "based *on*" something. For example, "My word-usage decision is based *on* accepted principles of English grammar."

---

[90] Some of these have appeared elsewhere in this book. Please forgive the repetition.

Using *irregardless* instead of *regardless*.

The latter is correct; the former is wrong, regardless of what many people say.

Writing sentences as run-ons.

A run-on sentence uses no periods—and often no punctuation at all—at the end of a complete thought (or independent clause) but keeps running on into the next sentence. For example, if you write (on Facebook, let's say), "On Christmas Eve we attended a wonderful church service following it we ate dinner," please know I'm grateful you shared that, but it took me an extra second or two to interpret it. Multiply that run-on sentence by several more in the same post, and you will bog down, confuse, and probably lose your reader (which definitely includes *me*). Punctuation is used to make writing more easy to read and comprehend. Using punctuation shows your reader that you care about them. Using punctuation is the loving thing to do.

Saying or writing *supposably* instead of *supposedly*.

The former means "capable of being supposed or conceived," but the latter is normally what people intend when they mean "assumed to be true," or "presumably." For example:

- "A dog may **supposably** be friends with a cat."
- "**Supposedly**, people who click on my blog page actually *read* my blog."

A common error with a related word is to use *suppose to* instead of the correct *supposed to,* as in, "I'm *supposed to* move on to the next grammar pet peeve before I lose my readers." Remember to add the *d*. The meaning of *supposed to* is something like "expected to."

Using *of* instead of *have*.

It's not "would of," "could of," or "should of." For example, "I would *of* done better in English class if I had paid attention" is incorrect. It should be, "I would *have* done better . . ." People make this mistake because they've heard the contraction *would've* and thought they were hearing would *of*. Nope. It's would *have*.

Neglecting to use a pair of commas to set off nonrestrictive noun appositives.

WAIT! Before you tune out, here's what I mean. (Please bear with me.) An appositive noun is a noun that follows a noun and gives additional information about that noun.

For example, "My boss, Hollingsworth, gave me a nice bonus for Christmas." *Hollingsworth* is the noun appositive, providing additional information about the word *boss*. It is considered to be nonrestrictive because the information (the name *Hollingsworth*) is not essential to the clear understanding of the sentence. The sentence would still make clear sense without it because who I mean by *my boss* is not grammatically restricted to *Hollingsworth*. Since I have only one boss, the name *Hollingsworth* gives additional information, but doesn't change the meaning of the sentence. It would make clear sense to say, "My boss gave me a nice bonus for Christmas." However, since I've decided to include the additional information of my boss's name, it must be set off with a **pair** of commas.

Now, if I had, say, three bosses—Hollingsworth, Betty Sue, and Billy Bob—I would need to punctuate that same sentence **without** commas: "My boss Hollingsworth gave me a nice bonus for Christmas." Writing it that way restricts what I mean by *boss* to one person and excludes Betty Sue and Billy Bob (who may have given me nothing—or maybe something else, like a nice rock), thus making *Hollingsworth* a restrictive noun appositive.

Remember, it's either a pair of commas or no commas. ONE comma doesn't work. I see this kind of error frequently: "My boss, Hollingsworth gave me a nice bonus for Christmas." What happened to the comma after Hollingsworth? And please remember to use that pair of commas if you're talking about your spouse: "For New Year's this year, my wife, Glenda, and I are staying home." If I forgot to set off *Glenda* with a pair of commas, you would have every reason to believe I had become a polygamist. For shame!

That's a whole lot of words to describe a relatively simple concept, but more words are just required.

Strange use of *concerning*

"Between a string of tourist deaths — and more being called into question as a result — plus the shooting of famed Boston Red Sox player David Ortiz, the Dominican Republic has been in the news for all the wrong reasons. **And it's concerning potential tourists**" (emphasis mine).[91]

The usage is awkward because "concerning"—a preposition— typically meant "regarding" or "about." ("The woman's question was concerning the soaring cost of groceries.") With that usage in mind, a reader will have to do a double take on the above news story: Was the shooting *regarding* potential tourists? Is it *about* potential tourists? No. The author meant it was *worrying* potential tourists, or it was *alarming* to potential tourists.

We have perfectly fine words to choose from when writing about worrisome or troubling topics. Let's use those, shall we?

"I have read and accept the terms and conditions."

I see this awkward construction all the time, and it makes my skin crawl. In fact, whenever I see one of these disclaimers written correctly, I'm almost bowled over. Can't these mega-corporations afford to hire someone familiar with grammar to proofread their website content?

---

[91] Retrieved 6/12/19 from https://www.yahoo.com/news/dominican-republic-faces-tourist-backlash-193952083.html. Author: David Oliver, *USA Today*

So how should it be written? Well, what do they want me to do? They want me to acknowledge two simple things: (1) that I **have read** the terms and conditions (which of course I almost never do), and (2) that I **accept** them or agree to them. That's all well and good, but if multiple verbs share a single subject (in this case, the subject is "I") the verbs should have the same tense, or the sentence isn't parallel.

Let's analyze it: The single subject, *I*, is followed by two verbs: "have read" (past participle) and "accept" (present tense). One grammarian asserted that, "If two or more ideas are parallel, they should be expressed in parallel grammatical form."[92] Parallel form requires that the verbs should have the same tense—preferably both past participles in this case: "I have read and have accepted," or simply, "I have read and accepted."

To keep the verb tenses as they are written, it should be written with two subjects—even if both subjects are the same—it just sounds better: "I have read and I accept the terms and conditions."

---

[92] Hacker 1985, 63.

Four Words and Expressions I Love to Hate

Do you ever cringe when you hear, or see in written text, a particular word or expression? Most people have their own private list of such terms. I know that I do. Here is my list of fingernails-scraping-the-chalkboard words and expressions that I wouldn't mind never hearing or seeing again.

1. Impacted (vs. affected) – over and over (and over) these days I hear or read impacted used, when *affected* or *influenced*—words that have served the purpose well for decades—are much better. Why turn *impact* into a verb? It's not necessary. Here's a recent example from an ad: "Do you know how your medications <u>impact</u> [read *affect*] your driving?"[93] And here's from an email announcement from a school district: "Governor Newsom has lifted the stay-at-home order for all regions of California, including the region where we live and work. While many of us are pleased to see a number of our local businesses opening up, this order does not <u>impact</u> [read *affect*] [our college's] plans for a safe, phased-in return."[94]

Why, why, *why* has "impact" come to supplant "affect" or "influence"? It has become a "vogue word," a linguistic fad, essentially. *Impact* has long been associated with phrases like, "The meteor made an impact on the topography," and "The missile exploded on impact." It's a word with some real oomph, stronger and sexier than the more blasé *affect*. So I understand what's happening, but *affect* is a perfectly fine verb, and *impact* should remain in the noun family. *Impact* as a verb connotes something much stronger than necessary most of the time, and its use is more cool, trendy, and voguish than it is necessary to convey meaning.

And then there's the dreadful and utterly unnecessary **impactful**, which may be one of the most awful adjectives of

---

[93] AAA ad received via email 11/18/19.
[94] Email received by author 1/27/21.

all time. Garner calls it "barbarous jargon."[95] Acceptable alternatives are, for example, *influential* and *powerful*.

2. Gift (noun used as a verb) vs. Give (the verb)

I read online recently that a well-to-do hip-hop singer gifted [read *gave*] his son an extremely expensive automobile for his sixteenth birthday. "Gave" is perfectly fine. It's one syllable and two letters shorter than "gifted," for one thing, and it just sounds more natural and less trendy. Is *gave* so run-of-the-mill, boring, and generic now? Perhaps.

How about another example: "Katharine Schwarzenegger, 29, gifted [read *gave*] [husband Chris] Pratt two pet pigs for his birthday that they named after country power couple Tim McGraw and Faith Hill."[96]

3. Confusing the back slash (\) and the forward slash (/) (Also called *diagonal, slant, solidus,* or *virgule.*)

Okay, this isn't exactly a word—but it still bugs me—in the context of URLs. For example, when I called the Social Security Administration recently, I got the recorded instructions about their phone menu. (Of course!) The lady's voice read the URL "www dot social security dot gov backslash benefits." Aargh! It's a stinkin' forward slash, dadgummit!

Here's how I keep it straight: when looking at a URL, reading left to right (as we do in English), I look at the slash. Is it leaning forward (to the right) or back (to the left)? If leaning to the right, it's a forward slash.[97] Easy-peasy, right?

---

[95] *Garner's Modern English Usage*, Fourth Edition 2016, 490.
[96] retrieved 7/1/19 from
https://www.foxnews.com/entertainment/katherine-schwarzenegger-chris-pratt-pet-pigs-tim-mcgraw-faith-hill
[97] As far as I know, all slashes in URLs are forward slashes. I'm sure I'll hear it if I'm wrong. (And that's okay.)

4. Missing or misused apostrophes in contractions and abbreviations.

When used in a contraction, an apostrophe substitutes or "stands in" for a missing letter or letters. Here are three examples:

- *Ma'am* is a contraction for *madam*, the apostrophe stands in for the missing *d*.

- *Rock 'n' roll*: the apostrophes substitute for two missing letters—*a* and *d*. Note that the apostrophe before the *n* is an *apostrophe* (') not an opening single quotation mark ('). There's a difference. Picky copyeditors notice things like that.

- When abbreviating years, an apostrophe stands in for the first two numerals of the year. I would say, *I graduated from high school in '89*—the apostrophe there is substituting for the missing *19*.[98] [99]

---

[98] As stated elsewhere, it's considered standard English to say, "graduated *from* high school" but not "graduated high school." The preposition *from* should be in there.

[99] I may or may not have graduated from high school in 1989.

Text or Texted . . . or *Texed*? Which Is It?

I was always amazed and secretly impressed when I walked across the college campuses where I worked for many years and saw young people sitting or standing, focus riveted on their cell phones held in two hands, with thumbs flying like greased lightning as they typed one text message after another. Me? I'm a one-finger texter, plodding along, one measly character at a time, always striving (ahem . . . of course!) for correct grammar and spelling.

It's now been more than 25 years since the word "text," referring to an electronic message sent from one cell phone to another, entered the English lexicon. Initially, "text" was always coupled with "message" and "text message" was simply a noun. We'd say, "I sent my friend a text message this morning about going to the concert on Saturday." It's natural for language to evolve over time and for verbal expressions to become more succinct. The phrase "send a text message" was shortened to "text" when we discovered it could serve nicely as a stand-alone verb. Now we say, informally, "I texted my friend this morning about going to the concert on Saturday." That is acceptable usage, and the dictionary even recognizes it.

Note that the verb "text" is a regular verb, meaning that it becomes past tense by adding *d* (if the word ends in *e*) or *ed* (as in this case). So how is it that I so often hear "text" used as the past tense of *text* in everyday spoken communication? "I *text* my friend this morning about going to the concert Saturday." Hold on there! What happened to the *-ed*?

This phenomenon is pervasive enough to deserve closer scrutiny. Why do so many of us drop the *−ed* from text when used as a past tense verb? I suppose one reason is that there isn't another word like it in the vernacular—no other *−ext* verb. (Are you aware of one?) But there is at least one *−ex* verb in use, which as a regular verb becomes past tense by adding *−ed*. I mean the word *vex*, which becomes past by adding *-ed*: *vexed*. Simple enough. But vex ends in *x*, not in *t*.

Whenever I hear the word *text* in the past tense, without the −*ed*, I can't help but think of *Texed*—because I tend to see words mentally when I hear them—and I wonder how the late

country-western singer Tex Ritter or the late baseball pitcher Tex Clevenger would feel about having their names twisted into some kind of past tense verb. To say, "I text you yesterday" (which

Tex Ritter

sounds like "Texed you") in that case would have to mean that yesterday I sang you a country and western song, or that I chucked a few baseballs at you.

So, to recap: *text*, used as a verb, is the present tense; *texted* (with the −*ed* tacked on) is the past tense, and is pronounced "tex-ted."

Okay, please excuse me while I go practice that.

"With That Being Said": An Annoying Expression

Here's how an email sent to all employees recently began:

Wow! July is right around the corner. With that being said, attached is the July newsletter for you to read and share.

"With that being said"? Huh?

It may be too kind to label "with that being said" as a cliché, but it is that at least. It should be labeled a hackneyed term,[100] or better yet, a nuisance. But because I want to be polite, I'll call it a cliché, and it's been around for a long time—many years. But lately it seems to be cropping up all over the place. Writers and speakers use it as a ready-made, no-bake transitional statement, along with its shorter cousins "having said that" and "that said." It's intended use is to smoothly shift gears from one sentence or one topic to the next, to shoehorn the reader (or listener) into what's to follow. It's a throwaway expression, a space-filler, and it generally adds nothing of substance to one's communications.

I'm picking on this cliché because of its frequent use in formal contexts—where the communicator has prepared an oral presentation, a paper, or a correspondence like the above email, in which careful thought was allegedly required. So what can we use to transition from one thought to the next without using this trite expression? Here are ten examples of common transitional expressions. Which one (or more) of these might work better than "with that being said"?

- *equally important*
- *in the same way*
- *as a result*
- *consequently*
- *for this reason*
- *therefore*
- *hence*
- *in any event*

---

[100] hackneyed (adj.): lacking in freshness or originality.

- *meanwhile*
- *however*

And perhaps the best transitional statement of all sometimes is . . . no transitional statement at all! Take that phrase out of the above email and see if it wouldn't be just peachy without it. Often, less is more—translated: fewer words frequently means better writing.

July is right around the corner. Attached is the July newsletter for you to read and share.

So, with that being said {cough} . . . let me quit this essay while I'm behind.

Pronoun Challenge – The Singular They

How should we refer to someone when we don't know, or aren't sure of, their gender? English does not have a common-sex singular personal pronoun. The latest print edition of the *Chicago Manual of Style* (the 17th) allows, with reluctance, the singular *they* when the gender is unknown or unspecified—as opposed to the troublesome *he or she* or equivalent construction—in speech and informal writing.[101] Although I tend to be conservative with the language, I have come to accept this.

Garner points out that the "indeterminate *they* is already more or less standard" for speakers of British English (BrE). He asserts that it "promises to be the ultimate solution to the problem" for speakers and writers of American English (AmE) as well.[102]

And it makes sense to me. For example, is there a more convenient way to articulate an announcement like this: "Someone left *their* car keys in the conference room after the meeting this morning. *They* may contact Betty Jean in the main office after lunch to retrieve them"?

Sometimes, "they"—although not perfect—is the best choice of pronouns. I recommend using it sparingly or it can easily draw attention to itself, which always diminishes clarity.[103]

---

[101] "They and their have become common in informal usage, but neither is considered fully acceptable in formal writing, though they are steadily gaining ground" (CMOS-17 2017, 5.256, 361).

[102] *Garner's Modern English Usage* 2016, 822.

[103] To be clear, please note that in this essay I am definitely neither referring to nor endorsing the current peculiar, voguish practice of naming and claiming one's very own personal pronouns and insisting that all of society applaud one's casuistry.

"Meme" – What Is It?

Lately, everyone seems to be creating memes, sharing memes, talking about memes, and commenting on memes in social media—but what in the world is a meme?

Meme, a neologism[104] that first appeared in the 1970s, is a behavior or an idea imitated or shared widely in a culture. Notice: a *behavior* or an *idea*, not a picture. The word, pronounced *meem*, is derived from the Greek word *miméme* ("same, alike"). It remained a fairly obscure word until the last few years, when the internet and social media infused it with new life. According to lexicographer Bryan Garner, a meme today is most often "a humorous video, phrase, illustration, or other symbol or depiction that is suddenly and widely spread by and mimicked or parodied on the Internet."[105] A meme in 2021 is typically a digital version of what we formerly called a poster or a graphic, and it contains a caption of some sort—often a quotation attributed to a person whose image is a featured part of the graphic.

The key thing that makes a meme a true meme, by definition, is that it is rapidly and widely shared in a culture or population via social media (like Facebook) on the internet. A person who makes his or her own illustration with a photo and a caption of some sort is not creating a "meme," unless it somehow catches on and goes viral, circling the globe faster than Superman. They are simply making a photo with a caption to share with friends.

---

[104] A neologism (nee-AH-luh-gizm) is a new or recently coined term.
[105] Bryan A. Garner, *Garner's Modern English Usage* (2016), 588.

Does the Sportscaster "Commentate"?

Recently, while watching the Olympics, I heard the announcer say that a certain colleague would be joining him to "commentate" during an upcoming event. Is *commentate* a word? Or is it just another sportscaster-created back-formation,[106] a jargon word that needlessly turns *commentator* into a verb? (Aren't you glad some people worry about these things so you don't have to?)

 According to reliable usage authorities, "commentate" is indeed a back-formation, and it dates from the late 18th century. It is not, however, considered a "needless variant," which would disqualify it from Standard English usage. Examples of needless-variant back-formations include *administrate* (a back-formation from *administration*—not needed because we have the perfectly fine verb *administer*) and *orientate* (a back-formation from *orientation*—not needed because we have the perfectly fine verb *orient*). Words like these and others (e.g., *interpretate, solicitate,* and *registrate*) do not accord with Standard English usage.

In the case of *commentate*, although a back-formation (from *commentator*), it is not a needless variant because the best alternative, *comment*, connotes brevity—as in "The official commented on the recent allegations." *Commentate* connotes a lengthier explanation or interpretation—which is what sportscasters often do. As one usage authority comments, "Some people dislike [commentate], but it has a specific context and serves a useful purpose."[107]

So go ahead and commentate. Although a bit of grandiose jargon, it is Standard English usage.

---

[106] Back-formations are most often verbs created from existing nouns. They are "formed by removing suffixes from longer words that are mistakenly assumed to be derivatives" (*Garner's Modern English Usage*, 2016, 90).

[107] Butterfield, *Fowler's Modern English Usage, 4th ed.*, 2015, 167.

Words Undervalued and Overvalued

Undervalued Words

Popular culture, which includes the realms of social media and text messaging, encourages us to undervalue words. Facebook (FB), for example, invited us to toss words into the dust bin when they created those cute little emoticons or emojis. What do the emoticons mean? *Like, Love, Ha-ha, Wow,* and *Angry*. The words—and underlying concepts—are virtually meaningless.

FB invites us to express supposed emotions with a single symbol, to save us the mental effort involved in using vocabulary to formulate sentences to express thoughtful replies. No need to do that when we can express displeasure by inserting an angry-face emoticon, or astonishment with a wow-face emoticon—when we may not feel anything like true anger or astonishment, in which case we're conveying pseudo-emotions. They're not real. And after a while, we almost lose the ability to distinguish between real and artificial feelings because we have lost the ability to articulate real feelings and ideas, because our mental processes have been trained to reduce everything to a single emoticon, which empties both the feelings and the words used to describe them of their meaning.

Sometimes the feelings involved are deep and genuine—I'm not suggesting we're all a bunch of phonies on social media (but many of us are a lot more unreal there than we care to admit). It's just that it's too easy to indicate that we "like" something, when what we really mean is that we acknowledge that we've seen it, or that we "love" something when what we actually mean is that we really *like* something or that something tugs heartstrings—not that we actually *love* it. Love is now almost a throwaway word, with no meaning. We love everything and everyone from our spouses to our next-door neighbor's new welcome mat.

In the same way that words like *awesome* and *amazing* have become meaningless through casual overuse. And of course, we all know how the world of text messaging has practically abolished literate written communication for many. "How r u? Hope ur better." "Thx im good." Come on, really? Communication practices birthed by the earliest texting technology have somehow carried over into the improved smart-phone technology, and yet not only do many people still use the "simplified" language in texts, but they also even use it in social media posts and in emails. An argument in its favor is that it's simpler, quicker, and easier, and that one's recipients can still decipher it. I get that. I studied human communication and general semantics in both undergraduate and graduate school[108] and have read a substantial amount of popular and scholarly literature on the subject of effective communication over the years.

My point is that literate written communication is under attack. Okay, perhaps that's too strong as it smacks of conspiracy theories and all that silliness. Literate written communication (and oral communication, for that matter) is in serious retrograde. Word meanings are dissolving into white noise and sentence construction is practically a lost art. For example, compare the writing of a typical high school or college student today to that of a typical farm kid with only a basic grammar school education one hundred or 150 years ago. Compare the clarity and depth of thought articulated through the vocabulary and syntax. It's interesting.

Overvalued Words

Our culture undervalues words by rendering them meaningless—especially on social media. But our culture contradicts itself by placing a much higher value on certain words than they deserve. Consider the words "outrage" and "offended." See how the media uses these words—how they cue us, the supposedly mindless sheep of the general public, on what to be offended and terribly angry about, to be "outraged" over. People aren't miffed, annoyed, upset, peeved, concerned, or even just angry anymore. That's not enough.

---

[108] I was one of those college students who couldn't make up his mind what he wanted to do when he grew up, so I majored in communication studies in both undergraduate and graduate school, not completing a degree in either.

Now they are *outraged*. Consider the recent controversy over Confederate statues. The media whipped up that frenzy to a hot flame, coaching us to suddenly feel offense and outrage, whereas prior to that no one gave a rat's behind about it.[109]

The same is true about almost everything today's protest industry gets worked up about. When you run an industry, you do your part to ensure its perpetuation through advertising and doing whatever you can to let the public know how much they "need" what you're selling. The protest industry has enlisted the mainstream media and social media to artificially inflate the importance of certain words and images in order to inflame our passions. There is a well-known word for that: propaganda.[110]

Today, young people are taught from an early age to be careful how they use certain words about certain subjects or people, because those words hurt people. That's good. We've improved as a society in that regard since my youth in the 1960s, when, for example, it was still mostly socially acceptable to use off-color terms for various ethnicities, the physically and mentally handicapped, and those of different sexual orientations. Ironically, it was okay to use those terms but totally taboo to use almost any curse word on television, in movies, in school, or in mixed company.

Today those taboos have been almost reversed. You mustn't disparage a person's identity (a good thing), but now you can curse away . . . like the guy sitting at the next table at the restaurant last week, whose every third word spoken to his buddies was the F-word. He wasn't whispering, and he didn't care how many women, children, men, or Martians overheard

---

[109] Make no mistake, I am not arguing in favor of Confederate statues. I'm simply pointing out how the media manipulates us so alarmingly effectively.

[110] I am fully aware of both the denotation and connotation of the word propaganda and of how the media today serves that purpose for the elites driving the prevailing narrative in society. For further reading, I recommend the classic *Propaganda: The Formation of Men's Attitudes* (1971), by Jacques Ellul and the outstanding *Speechless: Controlling Words, Controlling Minds* (2021), by Michael Knowles.

him. It was a normal part of his apparently vastly limited everyday vocabulary.

Today those taboos have been reversed. You can curse away . . . but don't dare call a Norwegian a Norsky.[111]

Six Rules for Effective Writing

1. *Never use a metaphor, simile, or other figure of speech that you are used to seeing in print.*

2. *Never use a long word where a short one will do.*

3. *If it is possible to cut a word out, always cut it out.*

4. *Never use the passive where you can use the active.*

5. *Never use a foreign phrase, a scientific word, or a jargon word if you can think of an everyday English equivalent.*

6. *Break any of these rules sooner than say anything outright barbarous.*

– George Orwell (1946)

---

[111] I am a Norsky, so I suppose I can write the word without being taken to task over it. Or *can* I?

Nineteenth Century Reading and Writing

America has always been a nation of readers. From the founding of the colonies in the seventeenth century, through the expansion of the western frontier in the early-to-mid nineteenth century, and well into the twentieth century, Americans cherished whatever printed matter they could get their hands on. For much of that history, for most citizens, that included at the very least the Bible and perhaps a handful of other publications, such as Noah Webster's *American Spelling Book* and the *McGuffey Reader*. The occasional newspaper was read from beginning to end, as were church denominational publications, such as the monthly *Millennial Harbinger* published by Alexander Campbell of the Disciples of Christ. The *Harbinger* was generally about thirty-two pages' worth of densely packed text with no illustrations. That's right—no photos, no drawings—nothing. Just text.

Subscribers looked forward to receiving the latest editions and would devour every word.

Americans of all socioeconomic stripes read novels as well, even though guardians of morality strenuously tried to discourage it as novels were deemed too "unreal" and put potentially tawdry images into the heads of impressionable youth and adults.

Personal letters were another source of reading material for many people, and they too were relished. If you wanted to communicate with someone who lived more than a few miles away, you had to write them a letter, which required you to sit down with pen and paper before you and give careful thought to the words and sentences you would write. This is why people who had perhaps only a grammar school education could read and write remarkably eloquent stuff. Letter writing—as writing in general—cultivates sharpness of thought.

Reading: Is Anything Better Than Nothing?

Does it matter what we read?

When it comes to children and young people reading, should parents/teachers/grandparents say, "I don't really care *what* they read, as long as they're reading"? I've heard folks say that many times through the years and never thought much of it. I tended to agree that kids reading *something* is better than reading *nothing*. And especially in this day of ubiquitous video games and various forms of electronic preoccupation, isn't it better for a kid to turn off the brain-numbing gadgets occasionally and exercise other intrapersonal proficiencies? And the same applies to adults: isn't it better to read *something* than nothing at all? With so many reading options available, from comic books to romance novels, to unlimited online content, what's the big deal? Just read *something*! Because reading, no matter what it is, is good for you.

But an article I read recently caused me to stop and reconsider that assertion. The author challenged the reading-something-is-better-than-reading-nothing thesis with the analogous, "I don't care what they're *eating* as long as they're eating." Read that clause again: "I don't care what they're eating as long as they're eating." He is implying, of course, that not all reading choices have equal value for enriching our lives and making us healthier, better people.

A pair of disclaimers are in order. **First**, I'm not talking about young children who are just learning to read, where the innate, God-given drive to learn and master one's world one step at a time brings the child (and his parents) a sense of accomplishment and joy. I do believe that any and every type of reading material that interests little tykes needs to be encouraged. I'm referring to older kids (and, yes, adults) who have gained some mastery of reading fundamentals, yet who, for whatever reason, don't read much.

Second, I'm excluding online content, including news, weather, sports, articles on assorted topics, and even blogs. For the most part, that sort of reading is ephemeral, meaning it's here today and gone tomorrow (or ten minutes from now).

And so, while that may be technically *reading*, it isn't the type of reading I'm talking about. I admit that, as much as I like to read in general, a sizable chunk of my reading these days consists of ephemera. And I worry that ephemera is producing an insidious shallowness in me. Reading twenty or thirty snippets of online content in one sitting on a regular basis may fool me into thinking I'm a well-informed person, but it may in fact be turning me into a Mississippi River kind of person: you know, someone who's a mile wide but an inch deep. That troubles me.

So how can we encourage our kids (and ourselves) to read *quality* material? One thing my wife and I have tried to do for both our kids and our grandkids is to stock our home library with quality children's and juvenile literature. This means forking out the money to acquire both the classics of yesteryear and the best writing of today. If you're new to this effort, an excellent place to start is Hillsdale College's "Classic Children's Literature" video series, where college instructors present overviews of beloved stories such as *Aesop's Fables, Beauty and the Beast, The Snow Queen, Alice's Adventures in Wonderland, Treasure Island,* and *The Wind in the Willows.*[112] I have watched the entire series, and it was well worth my time.

---

[112] For a great overview of Hillsdale College's free online course, go to https://online.hillsdale.edu/landing/classic-childrens-literature

Adult Literacy in the United States

Four in five U.S. adults (79 percent) have English literacy skills sufficient to complete tasks that require comparing and contrasting information, paraphrasing, or making low-level inferences— literacy skills at level 2 or above in PIAAC (OECD 2013). In contrast, one in five U.S. adults (21 percent) has difficulty completing these tasks. **This translates into 43.0 million U.S. adults who possess low literacy skills.** (My emphasis)

– Source: National Center for Education Statistics.[113]

Adults and Book Reading

A Pew Research Center report published in September 2021 revealed that one-quarter of U.S. adults have not read a book, or **even a portion of a book**, *in any form (print, e-book, or audio) in the past twelve months.*[114] (My emphasis)

---

[113] Retrieved 11/17/21 from
https://nces.ed.gov/pubs2019/2019179/index.asp
[114] Retrieved 11/16/21 from https://www.pewresearch.org/fact-tank/2021/09/21/who-doesnt-read-books-in-america/ft_2021-09-21_nonbookreaders_01/

How to Write Academic Degree Titles

Every year in May or June, hundreds of thousands of newly minted college grads wade into the sometimes turbulent, often murky, and always anxiety-producing waters of job hunting.

So let's think about how to correctly write academic degree titles on resumes, cover letters, and LinkedIn profiles. This can be confusing, and in my nearly twenty years in higher education, as a counselor, instructor, administrator, and hiring manager, I've seen many resumes and applications where the writer apparently didn't know how to identify his or her own degree. Stumbling over something so basic may not go over well with prospective employers. It never hurts to get this right.

To make it as simple as possible, I've put this information in chart form (and intentionally left the doctorate out of it as there are so many variations).[115]

Formal	Informal	Abbreviation
Associate of Arts/Science	associate degree	AA/AS
(or Associate in Arts/Science)	(note: **no** apostrophe)	
Bachelor of Arts/Science	bachelor's degree	BA/BS
	or bachelor's	
Master of Arts/Science	master's degree	MA/MS
	or master's	

NOTE that **informal** degree titles are **NOT CAPITALIZED** and that an **APOSTROPHE** (indicating possessive form) is used in *bachelor's* and *master's* but **not** *associate*.

---

[115] Sources consulted: *Chicago Manual of Style* (16th edition) and *The Associated Press Stylebook* (2017 edition).

Examples using the bachelor's degree:

CORRECT:

- **Formal:** *Adam has successfully completed his Bachelor of Arts in Economics.*

- **Informal:** *Adam has successfully completed his bachelor's (or bachelor's degree) in economics.* [Notes: (1) use an apostrophe; (2) the academic discipline is not capitalized unless the full formal degree title is used as above.]

- **Abbreviation:** *Adam has successfully completed his BA in economics.*

WRONG: *Adam has successfully completed his bachelor's of arts* (or *Bachelor's of Arts*) *in Economics.*

REALLY WRONG: *Adam has successfully completed his Bachelors of Arts in Economics* (or Bachelor's of Arts, or bachelors of arts) in Economics.

Examples using the master's degree:

CORRECT:

- **Formal:** *Eve earned a Master of Science in Business Administration in 1995.*

- **Informal:** *Eve earned a master's (or master's degree) in business administration in 1995.* [Notes: (1) use an apostrophe; (2) the academic discipline is not capitalized unless the full formal degree title is used as above.]

- **Abbreviation:** *Eve earned an MS in business administration in 1995.*

WRONG: *Eve earned a master's of arts (or Master's of Arts) in Business.*

REALLY WRONG: *Eve earned a Masters of Arts* (or *Masters, or masters of arts) in Business.*

Here's another tip: Please, please be sure to get your own field of study correct! For example, at many colleges and universities there's a "communication" or "human communication" (singular) degree, not "communications" (plural). If you write "communications," be sure that's what it's called at your school. Does it seem unimportant? Think again! If the competition for a position is stiff, every detail is especially important, and if you've claimed in your resume or cover letter that you "pay attention to details," it's doubly important.

Congratulations to ALL graduates and best wishes for your future endeavors.

By the way: One graduates *from* college; one doesn't "graduate college." The former is the preferred expression. ("I graduated from college in 1980). The latter is a common colloquialism ("I graduated college in 1980.") It should be avoided in formal writing. Remember to include *from*!

Eight Nonverbal Signals to Avoid Giving in a Job Interview

In my years as a student services professional and department manager at a large university, I was privileged to interview dozens of candidates for professional career positions and hundreds more for student-assistant jobs. Through those experiences, I learned what impresses interviewers and what turns them off. Interviews are nerve wracking, and most of us need all the help we can get to be at our best. That includes preparing for possible questions and being careful not to allow our nonverbal messages to overshadow our verbal messages and disqualify us from serious consideration. Avoid the following nonverbal signals.

1. Inappropriate grooming and dress, which signals lack of attention to detail.

This may seem obvious, but you need to dress and groom yourself appropriately for a job interview. Brush your hair, comb your teeth, shine your face, and wash your shoes—it's all important. Use mouthwash and don't forget deodorant. Go easy on the cologne or perfume—as hard as it is to believe, not everyone is enamored with the latest *eau de parfum*, and some may have allergies or upper respiratory conditions that could be set off by yours.

If it's a professional position or an office job, dress professionally. If it's a construction job, put on clean jeans and a clean work shirt. Individuality is a virtue and we all want you to express yourself, but on your own time. For the interview, dress the part. When in doubt, it's better to overdress than underdress.

2. Unsmiling facial expression, which signals unfriendliness.

"But I'm not a smiler," someone objects. Fine, fake it—especially in those first few moments when you're meeting the interviewers and getting settled into your chair. You need to let them know you are a friendly, interested person who's not going to bite. Pretend that you're the smilingest person in town on your way to a smiling convention. But remember to relax that smile when answering serious questions. Facial expressions appropriate for the questions are important. You don't want to be a grinning ninny. I'm not sure what that is, but you don't want to be one.

3. Lack of eye contact, which signals lack of confidence.

I've had job candidates actually look away from me while shaking my hand. They've already put themselves in a hole before the interview got started. Then during the interview they never looked at me, even when answering my questions; I felt like a dreaded Elephant Man. But eye contact is difficult for some of us. I can relate to the person who says, "I'm a shy person and it's hard to look strangers in the eye." Or, "In my native culture, we don't look authority figures in the eye." Or, "I'm so nervous, my knocking knees send out an involuntary SOS, and my eyes look unto the hills for deliverance."

I get the shy thing, I get the culture thing, and I get the scared, looking-to-the-hills thing, but at a job interview you need to get the "let's pretend" thing going. Let's pretend you're an actor playing a role—a role that could land you a truckload of money (or a coin purse full of coins—either way, some money)—and your role is to be Mr. or Ms. Confident. I don't mean Mr. or Ms. Pompous Jerk—I mean Mr. or Ms. *Warmly* Confident. Mentally command your eyes to keep fixed on the interviewer's eyes while introducing yourself or when he or she is asking questions. If there are other interviewers in the room, remember to look into each person's eyes occasionally, even when answering another's question; then go back to your questioner's eyes. It's impressive, and it expresses warm confidence.

4. Weak (or overly strong) handshake, which signals cluelessness.

Besides your confident eye contact and the smile on your face, your handshake is the next part of the first impression you make in a job interview. Be sure to avoid two extremes: the "limp fish" and the "vise-grip of death." The former says you're unenthusiastic or sick—or that you're still a clueless kid who hasn't learned grown-up things like how to shake hands; the latter says you're insensitive—a clueless brute who doesn't know his (or her) own strength, or you're a show-off trying to make people wince because you're a wee bit sadistic. Aim for a firm, but not too firm, handshake that communicates warmth, interest, confidence, and moderate enthusiasm.

5. Poor posture, which signals sloppiness.

One time we invited several internship candidates to come in for "informal" interviews, and we stressed the informal nature to help put the candidates at ease. One fellow was so informal that he slouched back in his chair, semi-reclined, while we asked him our questions. His body language, combined with his verbal answers, conveyed the message that he was not only sloppy but a bit too cool for the position—as if someone with half a brain could do the job with one eye closed and one hand tied behind his back. Did he get the position? I'll let you guess. Don't be disarmed if the hiring manager calls the interview "casual" or "informal." You still need to be on your toes and professional, with hair brushed and teeth combed—and for pity sakes, don't slouch back in your chair! Sit up straight and lean forward slightly.

6. Poor vocal performance, which signals insincerity.

I wasn't sure what to call this, but I'm talking about speaking too softly or too loudly; too slowly or too quickly; in a monotone or overly sing-songy. Within reason, speak as if you're telling a story to your friends. Use some inflection, pace yourself, speak clearly, pause appropriately, and when you're done, stop talking. Please.

Try not to be a giggling ninny—similar to the grinning ninny in number two above. If you giggle excessively when nervous, put a mental sock in it at the interview. A giggle or chuckle at appropriate moments conveys a cheerful disposition, which is a good thing. Incessant giggling in an interview conveys air-headedness, which is not a good thing. Be the most sincere version of "you" you can be.

7. Too much gesturing, which signals nervousness.

Some hand gesturing during an interview is okay if it fits what you're saying. It's hard to describe how big the fish you caught was without using your hands. But if it's just nervous, constant, willy-nilly gesturing—swatting at imaginary gnats—that's not okay. It's distracting. If you're not sure what to do with your hands, either keep them folded in front of you on the table, or, even better, folded in your lap. Keep gestures to a minimum.

8. Fiddling with something, which signals lack of awareness.

Along with the previous, one of the most distracting things to do with your hands is to constantly fiddle with papers, a folder, a pen, or some other physical object. I recall one candidate absentmindedly rolling and unrolling her resume and occasionally waving it around like a light saber. That sort of thing is a big distraction and will earn you big minus points. If you must bring a physical object to the interview, don't touch it until you absolutely need to—and take your hands off it when you're done with it. Pretend it's a hot potato that will sear the skin off your fingers if you pick it up. Be aware of where you are and what you're doing.

Keep these eight nonverbal behaviors at bay during your next interview, and good luck getting that great new job!

The Ever-Changing English Language

The changing/evolving English language. Need proof? How about the **Lord's Prayer** from circa 1000 A.D.:

> *Faeder ure,*
> *þu þe eart on heofonum,*
> *Si þin nama gehalgod.*
> *Tobcume þin rice.*
> *Gewurþe ðin willa on eorčan swa on heofonum.*
> *Urne gedaeghwamlican hlaf syle us to daeg.*
> *And forgyf us ur gyltas, swa we forgyfaõ Urum*
> *gyltendum.*
> *And ne gelaed þu on costnunge,*
> *Ac alys us of yfele. Soþlice.*

How many words can you identify? Maybe *Faeder ure*? (Our Father), *nama*? (name); *willa on eorčan*? (will [be done] on earth]; *And forgyf us . . . we forgyfaõ*? (forgive us . . . we forgive). Probably not much more, right? (Unless you've studied Old English—and I do know someone who has.)[116]

The point here should be obvious: English has evolved significantly over the centuries, and the evolutionary process continues as we speak. My goal as a grammar snoot isn't to capture the English of my youth—or my grandmother's youth——and freeze it for eternity. I recognize and appreciate the malleable nature of my native tongue. My goal in this book (and my online blog) however, is to identify its contemporary forms while advocating for (to borrow author Amy Einsohn's pithy phrase) "clarity, coherency, consistency, and correctness — in service of the 'Cardinal C': communication."[117] It's another way of saying what I put on the masthead of my website: "Celebrating Standard Written English and Effective Communication."

That's what it's all about.

---

[116] No, it's not me. It was one the instructors in my copyediting certificate program.
[117] Einsohn 2011, 3.

Chapter 7
English at the Holidays

Writing Presidents/President's/Presidents' Day

I would like to wish a happy birthday to George Washington, Abraham Lincoln, and all the presidents on their special day.

They neither know nor care that I have taken this moment to remember them. However, local businesses hoping to win our hard-earned dollars on that super-duper sale weekend care very much that our thoughts turn to them (I mean the *presidents*, of course, not the businesses).

Grammar buffs (I'd rather call them that than "grammar geeks," or "grammar nazis," or just plain "nerds") will pay attention to how holidays like this are written. That wasn't a problem when I was a kid in school with Half-Pint in the one-room schoolhouse on the Minnesota prairie because there was no Presidents Day; it was called Washington's Birthday (or Lincoln's Birthday) back then. In fact, Washington's Birthday still is the legal name for this federal holiday, although so many states have chosen to call it "Presidents Day" that we find that name most commonly.[118]

---

[118] The official government website gives this explanation: "This holiday is designated as 'Washington's Birthday.' Though other institutions such as state and local governments and private businesses may use other names, it is Federal policy to always refer to holidays by the names designated in the law." (http://www.archives.gov/news/federal-holidays.html)

Multiple Choice: How do you spell it? (Pay attention to apostrophe placement):

a) Presidents Day

b) President's Day

c) Presidents' Day

d) Either a or b is acceptable

e) Either a or c is acceptable

f) Who cares?

If you answered *e*, give yourself a Presidents' Day high-five. If you answered *f*, please step outside. I'll speak to you after class.

The mother style guide of all style guides in American English, the *Chicago Manual of Style* (17th ed.), instructs writers to spell it as a plural possessive (or genitive, if you prefer), with the concluding *s* followed by an apostrophe. The guide used for most journalistic publications, the *Associated Press Stylebook*, dictates the plural form without the apostrophe. If you see it spelled President's Day (singular possessive) you can know confidently, with grammar buffs everywhere, that it's wrong.

Don't be overly smug. A *little* smugness is okay.

What's So "Good" About Good Friday?

I suspect that many people—including the religious and nonreligious among us—are unclear as to why this day is called "Good Friday." Many folks at least vaguely realize it has some connection to Easter, that it has a "religious" meaning. But what makes it "good"? In some minds, it may be similar to Black Friday at Thanksgiving—a time to hit the stores (if they haven't already done so) and pick up all the last-minute goodies for Easter festivities: food, candy, plastic eggs, new outfits, and so forth. For some (before COVID-19 and forced home-stays) it was "good" because they got the afternoon off from work with pay, or the day off from school. But none of these things has anything to do with its true meaning.

If you google it, you can find a number of interesting explanations about the etymology of Good Friday. Here is the interpretation that I prefer: The church—meaning the collective body of people in the world who profess to believe in and follow Jesus Christ—has always understood that the greatest possible gift God bestowed upon humanity occurred on the day Christ was crucified on a cross nearly 2,000 years ago, the Friday of Passover week in c. 30 A.D.[119] This event in history, which occurred just outside of Jerusalem, is the sine qua non of the gospel message.[120]

---

[119] Some Bible teachers suggest Christ was crucified on Thursday, an opinion not shared by the majority of Christian scholars.

[120] Sine qua non – literally, *without which not*. It's something absolutely essential or indispensable – as the death, burial, and

Here is that gospel message in a nutshell, as most Christians understand it: "For God so loved the world that he gave his only begotten Son, that whosoever believeth in him should not perish, but have everlasting life" (John 3:16, KJV).

The death of Jesus Christ on that day in 30 A.D. effected the forgiveness of and liberation from the enslavement of sin of every person who believes and places their trust in him, repents of (turns away from) sin, and walks by faith in him. And for nearly 2,000 years, that has resulted in the greatest possible "good" for the greatest number of people in the history of the world. It brought hope to the world, the promise of eternal life with God in heaven, and true spiritual freedom.

During these fearful and uncertain days, we need this Good Friday message of forgiveness, and the hope we have through Christ's resurrection three days later (on Easter Sunday), more than ever.

---

resurrection of Jesus is indispensable to the gospel message, and, in turn, to the Christian faith.

Some Fourth of July Thoughts

How to write it: According to commonly accepted style conventions for formal English, official secular and religious holidays are written out and capitalized. Therefore we have *Fourth of July, July Fourth, the Fourth,* or *Independence Day* (note the four *e's* and no *a* in Independence). Of course, informally we can (and I do) write it *4th of July* or any way that others will understand.

Fascinating coincidence: Our second and third presidents (John Adams and Thomas Jefferson), who were both instrumental in the American Revolution and the founding of our country, died on the same day—July 4, 1826—the fiftieth anniversary of the signing of the Declaration of Independence.

Freedom, like anything else, has a cost. It is not free. It requires sacrifice, vigilance, and a courageous commitment to do what is right, even if what is right isn't popular.

Veterans Day

I salute all veterans of the US military. Thank you for your bravery and service.

Now, a brief word about **the proper way to write Veterans Day.** Many advertisers and individuals get this one wrong, placing an apostrophe between the *n* and *s*, hence making *Veteran's* Day a singular possessive, as if the day of recognition belonged to one specific veteran. What an honor to single out one veteran! Now, if the apostrophe were placed after the -*s*, hence *Veterans'* Day, that would indicate a plural possessive—a recognition belonging to all veterans. While much better, and grammatically correct, it still is not the preferred spelling, which is *Veterans* Day—with no apostrophe—the spelling used in the official statute establishing the legal holiday in 1954.

So why is *Veterans* (without an apostrophe) correct? Because it's an **attributive noun.** Amy Einshon explains it this way: "The apostrophe is sometimes omitted when a plural head noun ending in *s* functions as an adjective rather than as a possessor; in other words, when the relations between the plural head noun and the second noun could be expressed by the prepositions 'for' or 'by' rather than the possessive 'of.'"[121]

So, to put into layman's terms, since it is meant that the holiday is a day *for* veterans, rather than a day *belonging* to veterans, we use the plural form and omit the apostrophe. The same thing applies to *carpenters union, teachers association,* and *farmers market:* a union *for* carpenters, an association *for* teachers, and a market *for* or *by* farmers.

I suspect we will see Veterans Day appearing in all three versions (attributive noun, plural possessive, and singular possessive). But you can let all your friends know which is correct.

---

[121] Einsohn 2011, 137.

Five Thanksgiving Words

We celebrate Thanksgiving Day on the fourth Thursday of November each year. I thought it would be fun to investigate  the origins of several words commonly associated with the holiday. Enjoy![122]

Thank comes from the Old English word *thanc*, which is derived from the prehistoric Germanic *thangk*, with a root idea of thought or thoughtfulness. The English word *think* comes from the same root. It's easy to see how our word for expressing gratitude originated from the concept of thinking or giving thoughtful consideration. To give thanks is to think about and express one's gratitude for something. And what better way to say "thank you" than by enjoying a big feast?

Feast. While we usually think of a feast as "an elaborate and usually abundant meal often accompanied by a ceremony or entertainment," the word originated in the Latin *festus*, which meant "joyful" or "merry," and our words *festival* and *festivity* are derived from it. In the early church, Christmas (or the Feast of the Nativity) and Easter were just two of the festivals observed by Christians—occasions of joyful celebration that included abundant eating—usually after a time of fasting and solemn reflection. Over time, abundant meals themselves, for whatever occasion, became simply *feasts*. On a side note, Christmas is a "fixed feast" (always celebrated here in the West on December 25th); Easter is a "moveable feast," meaning its date varies. It is observed on the first Sunday after the first full moon after the beginning of spring.) Thanksgiving Day, then, is also a moveable feast as it is

---

[122] Sources: John Ayto, *Dictionary of Word Origins* (New York: Arcade Publishing, 1990); *Merriam-Webster's Collegiate Dictionary*, 11th ed. 2009).

celebrated in America on the fourth Thursday of November. In Canada, it is the second Monday in October. The Jewish Passover is also a moveable feast. What Thanksgiving feast would be complete without turkey?

Turkey. Did you ever associate the name of the large fowl with the country of Turkey? If so, you were probably right. Originally, *turkey* referred to the "guinea-fowl," a bird imported to Europe by the Portuguese from Africa by way of the Turkish territory. It is said that when the bird we in America now know as the turkey was introduced in the 16th century to the British, it reminded them of their "turkey," the guinea-fowl, so they began to call the larger American bird by the same name. Therefore, yes: there is a loose connection between the country of Turkey and the large bird consumed by the millions on Thanksgiving Day. And how many bazillion potatoes are consumed on Thanksgiving?

Potato. In English, the first *potato* was the sweet potato. Shakespeare, in *The Merry Wives of Windsor* (1598), had Falstaff say, "Let the sky rain potatoes!" He was referring to sweet potatoes, which supposedly had aphrodisiac properties. At the end of the sixteenth century, the word *potato* first came into use for the vegetable we now know by that name. The word was derived from the Spanish *patata*—from the Taino language (Caribbean region) word *batata*—for sweet potato. So enjoy whichever type of potato you choose on Thanksgiving, but don't forget the pumpkin pie for dessert.

Pumpkin. What do pumpkins and pom-poms have in common? Etymologically, the round, brightly colored ball-shaped thing we call a *pom-pom* and the *pumpkin* can be traced back to the French *pompon*, which resulted from the

Greek *pepon*: a type of melon that was not eaten until it was

fully ripe. So the big, round, ripe Greek *pepon* became the French *pompon*, which became the English *pompion* in the sixteenth century, and eventually the *-ion* ending became *-kin* (*pompkin*), and then finally *pumpkin*. Enjoy your pie.

Next Thanksgiving, remember to think about and thank the One to whom the pilgrims gave thanks nearly four centuries ago. We all have many blessings to count.

How to Sign Holiday Greetings & Gift Cards

How do you sign a card or gift tag when you want to say it's from you, your spouse, the kids, and the dog (okay, even from the cat)? That is, the entire [insert appropriate name] family. Specifically, where do you put the stinking apostrophe? Or *is* there an apostrophe? That's the $64,000 question.

The Rule

Ah, the apostrophe: blessing to some and bane to many. Let's have a quick review of its three basic uses: (1) to indicate possession ("the *Christensens'* home"); (2) to make a contraction ("*Isn't* that nice?" "I *don't* care."); and (3) in certain rare occasions to avoid confusion, to indicate plural ("Here are the *do's* and don'ts of apostrophe use."). Apart from the rare number 3, apostrophes do *not* a plural make.

Let me say it another way: Adding apostrophe *s* to a word does not make it plural. In 99.99 percent of its uses, the apostrophe indicates possession or a contraction of two words into one, not a plural.[123] Have I made that point clear, that we don't add an apostrophe *s* (or *s* apostrophe) to a word or name to make it plural?

The Quiz

So let's look at the graphic to the right and decide which one is correct. Is it:

(a) *Merry Christmas from the Christensen's,*

(b) *Merry Christmas from the Christensens',* or

(c) *Merry Christmas from the Christensens?*

---

[123] This 99.99% statistic is based on observation and semi-educated conjecture. In other words, I made it up—but it seems about right.

Contestants, you have 30 seconds to write your answers. [Hum *Jeopardy* music here.]

If you answered (c), *Merry Christmas from the Christensens* (no apostrophe), you win! Your $64,000 check is in the mail.

This is also correct if you are giving a card or gift *to* the Christensens (again, no apostrophe). The Christensens includes me, my wife, the kids, the dog, and anyone else who wants to claim kinship. No apostrophe. No apostrophe. No apostrophe. I feel like I'm repeating myself.

The Exception

Not to confuse you (you knew I'd try), but there is a time when you do appropriately include an apostrophe: when you are sending an invitation to an event or writing directions to your place. So if you send me an invitation to join your family for a holiday party, and your name is Brown, you would write, *Come enjoy a holiday party at the Browns'*. And when writing out directions, you would say, *Here's how to get to the Browns'*.

Why the apostrophe now, for pity's sake? Because in both instances you're indicating a possessive and the word *place* is implied: *Come enjoy a holiday party at the Browns' [place]*. *Here's how to get to the Browns' [place]*. If there's only one of you, you might write, *Here's how to get to Brown's [place]*, although you'd probably say *my place*, or *Dan Brown's house*. (You'll need to crack the elusive code at the gate to get in.)

If your name ends in s or z, you will typically add *es* to make it plural. For example, *Merry Christmas! With love, the Joneses* (note the *es* to make it plural—and no apostrophe). Or if it's an invitation: *You're invited to the Martinezes' for a New Year's bash!* (it's plural, so the *es* is needed, and again the word *place* is implied, so we add the apostrophe to make it possessive).

Ten Christmas Terms Explained

Do you know where all ten of the following Christmas terms came from?

1. Advent – Advent is derived from the Latin *adventus*, meaning "arrival" or "the coming." By the end of the sixth century, Pope Gregory I had instituted in the Roman church the practice of conducting a special mass on each of the four Sundays leading up to "the coming" of the Christ-child. Similar to Lent, the season of Advent included fasting and penitence followed by a time of celebration. Eventually, the penitential nature of Advent gave way exclusively to the celebratory nature. Today, Advent is still celebrated in many churches, with each Sunday featuring a different theme, such as the prophecies of Jesus' birth, the Annunciation to Mary, the visitation of the angels and shepherds, or the gifts of the wise men—with a candle lit for each theme.

2. Carol – Singing Christmas carols in church or outside of people's homes is a favorite tradition of many. A term in use since the 14th century, a *carol* is typically a joyful religious song, slightly less formal than a hymn, and sung outside the four walls of the church. Carols today are closely identified with the celebration of Christ's birth. The word has been used in verb form since the 14th century as well—"Here we come a caroling..."

3. Wise Men (or magi – from Greek *magoi* – μάγοι) – The King James Version refers to the magi as "wise men." The Greek word, *magoi*, refers to the unnumbered and unnamed pagan astrologers who, as reported in Matthew's Gospel, arrived "from the east"—probably Persia or Babylonia—to pay homage to the baby Jesus, presenting him with gifts of gold, frankincense, and myrrh. As influential men of learning, they were certainly "wise men," and thus the translation. Today, the magi (wise men) are immortalized in Nativity scenes and in carols, such as "We Three Kings of Orient Are." Although the legend that the magi were *kings* has been around since the fifth century, there is no biblical or other convincing evidence to substantiate it.

4. Gay (as in "don we now our gay apparel" and "make the yuletide gay") – Young people today may not know that "gay" once had nothing to do with sexual orientation. It's original meaning was "lively" or "brightly colored," and that was predominantly how it was used until the 1970s. Although Merriam-Webster's Collegiate Dictionary still lists the older definition as the primary one, the American Heritage Dictionary, along with most current usage guides, lists the newer meaning as current. It is what it is. But when we sing "Deck the halls with boughs of holly . . . don we now our gay apparel," we are using the older meaning.

5. Yule (yule log and yuletide) – This term is rooted in the ancient Norse feast of "Midwinter." As Christianity began to take over the Scandinavian region in the sixth and seventh centuries, it infused new meaning in the Norse feast and soon the festival celebrating Christ's birth was called simply *Jul* (Yule in English). The meaning of the word is unclear. But when we hear "yule log" and "yuletide" we can mentally substitute "Christmas log" and "Christmastide."

6. Twelve Days of Christmas – The twelve days of Christmas are December 25 (Christmas day) through January 6 (Epiphany). If you count the days, you will come up with thirteen. The best information I could uncover is that the first day, Christmas, is often not counted in the twelve days, so by the time we get to January 6, that day is considered Day Twelve. However the counting is done, the Twelve Days has been recognized by many Christians as a part of the celebration of Christ's birth—and his baptism (Epiphany)—for centuries. The song "The Twelve Days of Christmas," which has been around for centuries in one form or another, features a series of silly gifts given to one's "true love" over that twelve-day span. A mathematics professor noted in a 1959 journal article that if one adds up all the gifts given over the twelve days, the total is 364, with the speculation that the lover has provided his or her beloved with a gift for each day of the upcoming year. On the 365th day—Christmas day—

Christ himself is the greatest gift of all. True? Who knows, but the speculation is interesting.

7. Calling birds – While on the topic of the Twelve Days of Christmas, on day four the true love gives "four calling birds." According to reliable historical sources, the lyric was originally "four *colly* birds," which derives from the Old English word *col*, or coal. A "colly bird," then was a black-colored bird, or a blackbird. In Medieval times, blackbirds (and other kinds of birds, like French hens, turtle doves, and partridges) were considered a tasty delicacy to be baked into a pie. Yum![124]

8. Nativity – This word has its origins in the Latin *nativus*—birth. In English it is usually capitalized and preceded by the definite article—*The Nativity*—and refers to the birth of Jesus Christ. The earliest Christians did not celebrate the birth of Christ until the middle of the fourth century, and then it was known as the Feast of the Nativity.[125]

9. Christmas – The Roman church celebrated Christ's birth (Advent, The Nativity) with a special midnight mass for centuries before it was first known in England as *Christes maesse* (or Christ's mass) in the eleventh century—probably around 1050 A.D. Eventually, it simply became *Christmas*. Within a hundred years, we find evidence of Christmas being spelled with an *X* (*Xmas*). Why?

10. Xmas – When I was a young boy, my mother, a devout Christian woman, made it clear to me that Christmas should never be spelled *Xmas* because, according to her understanding, *X* indicated an unknown quantity (as in algebraic equations). It was therefore borderline blasphemy to refer to Jesus Christ as an "unknown." Pagans might use

---

[124] Or *yuck*, depending on one's tastes.

[125] I'm tremendously condensing this account and leaving out details, such as how the Western church settled on December 25 as the day of Christ's birth and how and when the first feasts of the Nativity began.

Xmas, but not Christians. Although I learned a different way to understand *Xmas* when I grew up—and discovered it wasn't as sinister as my mother believed it to be—I still don't spell it that way. Here's the background: In the sixteenth century, Englishmen who had studied Greek learned that, in that language, Christ is spelled Χρίστος (*Christos*).[126] Some of them started using the first letter, *X* (or chi—pronounced *kye*), as shorthand for Christ. From there, it was a short step for Christmas to become *Xmas*. In the 20th century, advertisers learned that *Xmas* was a nice, short, space-saving abbreviation of *Christmas*, and so it entered popular culture.

Dictionaries and usage guides generally advise pronouncing *Xmas* as *Christmas* (not *ecksmas*), but I can't help it—when I see *Xmas*, in my head I hear *ecksmas*. In formal writing we should avoid this abbreviated form. And while I don't attribute sinister motives to those who use it informally, I will never be able to bring myself to use "Xmas," because it appears—at least *appears*—to remove Christ from Christmas.[127]

---

[126] Keep in mind that the New Testament was originally written in Greek.

[127] Sources used for this essay: Kelly, Joseph F. *The Origins of Christmas*. Collegeville, MN: Liturgical Press, 2004.; Miles, Clement A. *Christmas Customs and Traditions*. New York: Dover Publications, 1976 reprint of original 1912 edition; Grant, Leigh. *Twelve Days of Christmas: A Celebration and History*. New York: Harry N. Abrams, 1995; Riker, William H. *A Note on Numerology in "The Twelve Days of Christmas."* The Journal of American Folklore, Vol 72 (Oct-Dec, 1959), 348; Garner, Bryan A. *Garner's Modern English Usage, 4th ed.* Oxford: University Press, 2016.

An Ungrammatical Christmas Story

To celebrate the Christmas season, I once wrote a simple, quirky, short story containing many grammatical errors. Some are easy to spot; others require closer inspection. See how many you can find. The answer key is below (no cheating!) with corrections in **bold**. The errors are fairly straightforward, and involve mainly punctuation, spelling, and grammar.

Once upon a time a we Lad and lass lived in a little house by the lane. The lads name was Laddie and the lasses name was Mavis, but Laddie called her Lassie. One Christmas as they looked out on the Feast of Stephen, the snow laid round about—deep crisp and even, a poor man came in view gathering Winter fuel. He looked so much like their uncle but may have been jolly old saint Nicholas. They hoped that soon he would join there family in the nice warm house to roast chessnuts on a open fire.

"Its the most wonderful time of the year", said Laddie to Lassie. "Soon . Santa Clause will bring you and I nice present's."

"It's the hap-happyest season of all!" Lassie stammered in her exitement. "Lets lay down our head's for a long Winters nap. It won't be to long before Santa is here". So they went and laid on there beds.

It was a silent night and a holy night, the stars brightly shining. It was like the night of their deer saviors birth. All of the sudden, they heard a big clatter. Ran to the window to see what was the matter. it was only their Uncle dashing through the snow in a one-horse open slay jingling bells all the way.

He looked up and saw Laddie and Lassie gazeing out the Window at him, he shouted, "Merry Christmas children! And to all a goodnight!"

Laddie and Lassie couldn't tell for sure but they thought they heard him say "Ho ho," and they thought they saw his belly shake like a bowl full of Jell-O® brand figgy pudding. It may have been only their imagination . . . only their imagination.

Soon they fell asleep and dreamed about dancing sugar plums. They had never saw real sugar plums before—let alone dancing one's—so what they saw in their dreams looked kind of like powdered sugar donut holes.

Here's the way I corrected (or copyedited) the story:

Once upon a time, a **wee l**ad and **l**ass lived in a little house by the lane. The lad's name was Laddie and the **lass's** name was Mavis, but Laddie called her Lassie. One Christmas as they looked out on the Feast of Stephen, the snow **lay** round about—deep, crisp, and even. **A** poor man came in view gathering **w**inter fuel. He looked so much like their uncle, but may have been jolly old **S**aint Nicholas. They hoped that soon he would join **their** family in the nice, warm house to roast chestnuts on a**n** open fire.

"It's the most wonderful time of the year," said Laddie to Lassie. "Soon, Santa **Claus** will bring you and **me** nice **presents**."

"It's the hap-happ**i**est season of all!" Lassie stammered in her ex**c**itement. "Let's lay down our **heads** for a long **w**inter's nap. It won't be to**o** long before Santa is here.**"** So they went and **lay** on **their** beds.

It was a silent night and a holy night**.** The stars **were** brightly shining. It was like the night of their de**a**r **S**avior's birth. All of **a** sudden, they heard a big clatter**, and r**an to the window to see what was the matter. It was only their **u**ncle dashing through the snow in a one-horse open **sleigh,** jingling bells all the way.

He looked up and saw Laddie and Lassie **gazing** out the window at him. **H**e shouted, "Merry Christmas, children! And to all a goodnight!"

Laddie and Lassie couldn't tell for sure, but they thought they heard him say, "Ho ho," and they thought they saw his belly shake like a bowl full of Jell-O® brand figgy pudding. It may have been only their imagination . . . only their imagination.

Soon they fell asleep and dreamed about dancing sugar plums. They had never **seen** real sugar plums before—let alone dancing ones—so what they saw in their dreams looked kind of like powdered sugar donut holes.

So how did you do? There are about fifty corrections. Did you miss anything? Did I? Let me know.

"Auld Lang Syne" on New Year's Eve

What do the famous lyrics mean?

"We'll take a cup of kindness yet, for auld lang syne."

Each year, when we ring down the curtain on yet another year, many of us will hear, play, or sing what is sometimes dubbed "the most famous song that nobody knows." With lyrics traditionally butchered by millions at midnight on New Year's Eve—"Auld Lang Syne" was the title and key phrase of a Scots poem written by Robert Burns in 1788. The phrase itself had been around for 200 years before Burns's poem popularized it.

"Auld lang syne" ("syne" can be pronounced either "zine" or "sine") translates literally into English as "old long since" and means essentially "days gone by" or "long, long ago." It's historically a drinking song—the phrase "we'll take a cup of kindness" isn't referring to warm milk—but feel free to enjoy it without alcohol. It suggests reminiscing about good times with old friends and loved ones that we promise never to forget. "Should old acquaintance be forgot?" *Never!* is the implied answer. The song has five verses, but no one sings— or shall I say *attempts* to sing—anything but the first verse and the chorus, which follows:

> *Should auld acquaintance be forgot,*
> *and never brought to mind?*
> *Should old acquaintance be forgot,*
> *and auld lang syne?*
>
> *CHORUS:*
> *For auld lang syne, my dear,*
> *for auld lang syne,*
> *we'll take a cup of kindness yet,*
> *for auld lang syne.*

Aside from countless movies in which the song has been used (my favorite is the final scene of *It's a Wonderful Life*) and many recordings by popular artists, no one did more to embed the song in popular American culture than Guy Lombardo and his Royal Canadians. My older readers will certainly remember him. Lombardo's entertainment was the nation's New Year's Eve staple on radio and television for nearly fifty years during the mid-twentieth century, and "Auld Lang Syne" always accompanied the stroke of midnight.

Concluding Thoughts

Could I have included material on more topics in these pages? Obviously, I could. In fact, multiply these pages tenfold and we'd only be scratching the surface. I do hope, however, that this little book has been helpful to some degree, or thought-provoking, or mildly entertaining, or even irritating at times.

If you purchased it online, your rating and review would be greatly appreciated, and recommending—or giving it—to your friends and family would be as well.

If you would like to reach me with comments, corrections (heaven forbid!), or even suggestions for a future book, please send an email to Dean@TheDeansEnglish.com.

As popular artist Bob Ross used to say at the conclusion of his half-hour television programs, I say to you:

God bless, my friend.

Appendix
Are Copyeditors Needed in the 21st Century?

I read an article online recently posted by a Christian web magazine that, well, needed some copyediting. The author's bio stated that he (the writer) was a minister who had written and published several books on a variety of topics allegedly of interest to Christians. Because of an almost obsessive curiosity about such things, I decided to click a hyperlink to get more info. It took me to the author's page on Amazon and to a half-dozen titles he had penned. I clicked on one of them and discovered quickly that it had been self-published. No problem there at all. I have copyedited a number of books for writers who have published their own work and self-publishing is, to borrow a great Leonardo Di Caprio line from the *Aviator*, "the way of the *future*; the way of the *future*; the way of the *future*."

Good grammar is like personal hygiene - you can ignore it if you want, but don't be surprised when people draw their conclusions.

your e cards

But the danger in self-publishing is that the quality of the finished product may be substandard, which reflects poorly on the writer. The author in question, for example, had a missing word or two in the bio on the back cover of his book; every page I perused in the "Look Inside" sneak peek had problems—whether missing or misused punctuation, missing or misspelled words, clunky syntax, or clumsy word usage—which made reading a chore instead of a pleasure and severely diminished the author's credibility and my opinion of his competence.

Did he use the services of a copyeditor or even a proofreader? It didn't appear so, and if so, he or she didn't do a good job.

So what, exactly, does a copyeditor do? Read on.

The Copyediting Process

A copyeditor's job is to take an author's written document and ensure that it is **clear, concise, coherent, and correct.** I often say that a good copyeditor will make an author's piece shine a little brighter (and in some cases a *lot* brighter).

Here are the main categories of things I have looked for when copyediting articles, book manuscripts, theses, essays, cover letters, and website content for many clients:

- **Style** – Making sure the overall style conforms to an appropriate style guide, such as Chicago, MLA, APA, or AP. If none is specified,

- **Grammar** – Ensuring that the material is grammatically correct, according to widely accepted conventions of Standard Written English.

- **Punctuation** – Checking for the proper use of commas, semicolons, quotation marks, periods, apostrophes, dashes, hyphens, parentheses, etc.

- **Usage** – Are words used according to the conventions of Standard Written English?

- **Spelling** – Not relying on spell-check, but checking for spelling consistency, variants, homonyms, etc.

- **Syntax** – I call this the **"readability factor."** How are sentences and paragraphs organized? Are they as clear and concise as possible?

- **Capitalization** – Making sure words that should be capitalized are and those that shouldn't aren't.

- **Formatting** – Of footnotes, the bibliography, numbers, lists, tables, front matter, back matter, word and line spacing, etc., as requested by the author.

- **Point of view** – Checking for consistency and appropriateness.

- **Conciseness** – Minimizing the wordiness to maximize the message. This is especially important when it comes to website content.

- **Factual errors** – The heaviest burden of fact checking falls on the author's shoulders, but where obvious or possible errors have occurred, I query the author.

- **Legal requirements** – Ensuring, to the best of my knowledge, that sources are properly cited and that permissions are secured for copyrighted materials used. The final responsibility for these things lies with the author and publisher.

Please seriously consider employing the services of a professional copyeditor for your next important writing project.

Acknowledgements

I hope you enjoyed this book and find that it helps you communicate in writing more clearly and effectively, and brings you enjoyment in the process. I welcome your questions and comments.

I am indebted to my parents, who instilled in me a respect for and appreciation of grammar from an early age. My mother was a Midwest farmer's daughter and Midwest farmer's wife with only a high school education (valedictorian, class of 1930), but that education included courses in English and Latin. Her first spoken language was Norwegian. Her mother, my grandmother, was a schoolteacher for several years before marrying my grandfather, a farmer. She had taken four years of Latin in high school in a rural community in the Midwest (class of 1909). Love for language, and English in particular, is in my DNA.

My wife, Glenda, put up with my many hours holed up in my study at home writing, rewriting, and revising this manuscript. An avid reader, she is also gifted in written-English skills. She graciously read and proofread this manuscript and suggested many improvements, for which I am most grateful. She also helped tremendously with the cover design. Any remaining errors, typos, or "dummos" herein are solely my responsibility.

Unsurprisingly, our grown children, college graduates, are masterful writers and wordsmiths in their own right. I am thankful that they are rearing children (our grandchildren) who love—or *will* love when old enough—reading and writing. That love, along with a vibrant religious faith modeled in the home, is crucial to success in family relationships, academic success, and life in general.

Bibliography

Alward, Edgar C., and Jean A. Alward. 1997. *Punctuation Plain & Simple*. New York: Barnes & Noble.

Ayto, John. 1990. *Dictionary of Word Origins*. New York: Arcade Publishing.

Baer, Drake. 2016. "The Unexpectedly Existential Roots of Adjective Order." *The Cut*, September 7. Accessed November 28, 2017. https://www.thecut.com/2016/09/the-unexpectedly-existential-roots-of-adjective-order.html.

Bernstein, Theodore M. 1965. *The Careful Writer: A Modern Guide to English Usage*. New York: Atheneum.

Brians, Paul. 2013. *Common Errors in English Usage*. Portland, Oregon: William, James & Co.

Burchfield, R. W., ed. 1996. *The New Fowler's Modern English Usage*. Third. Oxford: Oxford University Press.

Casagrande, June. 2014. *The Best Punctuation Book, Period*. Berkeley, CA: 10 Speed Press.

Clark, Roy Peter. 2010. *The Glamour of Grammar: A Guide to the Magic and Mystery of Practical English*. New York: Little, Brown and Company.

Curme, George O. 1947. *English Grammar*. New York: Barnes & Noble Books.

Daniels, Barbara J., and David I. Daniels. 1991. *HarperCollins College Outline: English Grammar*. New York: Harper Perennial.

Einsohn, Amy. 2011. *The Copyeditor's Handbook: A Guide for Book Publishing and Corporate*

Communications. Third. Berkeley, CA: University of California Press.

Fay, David, and Anne Cutler. 1977. "Malapropisms and the Structure of the Mental Lexicon." *Linguistic Inquiry* (MIT Press) 8 (3): 505-520. Accessed August 22, 2019. https://www.jstor.org/stable/4177997.

Fernald, James C. 1916. *English Grammar Simplified*. Second. New York: Funk & Wagnalls Co.

Flesch, Rudolf. 1949. *The Art of Readable Writing*. New York: Harper & Brothers Publishers.

Forsyth, Mark. 2014. *The Elements of Eloquence: How to Turn the Perfect English Phrase*. London: Icon Books Ltd.

Fowler, H. W. 2009. *A Dictionary of Modern English Usage: The Classic First Edition*. Edited by David Crystal. New York: Oxford University Press.

Fowler, H. W., and F. G. Fowler. 1906, 2003. *The King's English (Reprint)*. Third. New York: Oxford University Press.

Froke, Paula, Anna Jo Bratton, Oskar Garcia, David Minthorn, Karl Ritter, and Jerry Schwartz, . 2017. *The Associated Press Stylebook and Briefing on Media Law 2017*. New York: Basic Books.

Fromkin, Victoria A. 1973. "Slips of the Tongue." *Scientific American* 229 (6): 110-117. Accessed September 11, 2019. https://www.jstor.org/stable/10.2307/24923270.

Garner, Bryan A. 2016. *Garner's Modern English Usage, Fourth Edition*. New York: Oxford University Press.

—. 2016. *The Chicago Guide to Grammar, Usage, and Punctuation*. Chicago: The University of Chicago Press.

Good, C. Edward. 2002. *Who's (...Oops!) Whose Grammar Book Is This Anyway?: All the Grammar You Need to Succeed in Life*. New York: Barnes & Noble Books.

Gunner, Jennifer. n.d. *Your Dictionary*. Accessed November 11, 2021. https://examples.yourdictionary.com/examples-of-puns.html.

Hacker, Diana. 1985. *Rules for Writers*. New York: St. Martin's Press.

Hale, Constance. 1999. *Sin and Syntax: How to Craft Wickedly Effective Prose*. New York: Three Rivers Press.

—. 2012. *Vex, Hex, Smash, Smooch: Let Verbs Power Your Writing*. New York: W.W. Norton & Company.

Hudson, Robert, ed. 2004. *Christian Writer's Manual of Style*. Grand Rapids, Michigan: Zondervan.

King, Stephen. 2000. *On Writing: A Memoir of the Craft*. New York: Scribner.

Lance, Donald M. 1977. "What Is "Grammar"?" *English Education* (National Council of Teachers of English) 9 (1): 43-49. Accessed June 13, 2016. https://www.jstor.org/stable/40172198.

LaRocque, Paula. 2003. *The Book on Writing: The Ultimate Guide to Writing Well*. Arlington, TX: Grey and Guvnor Press.

Le Peau, Andrew T. 2019. *Write Better: A Lifelong Editor on Craft, Art, and Spirituality*. Downers Grove, Illinois: InterVarsity Press.

Lederer, Richard. 1981. "A Primer of Puns." *The English Journal* (National Council of Teachers of English) 70 (6): 32-36. Accessed September 11, 2019. https://www.jstor.org/stable/817149.

Leggett, Glenn, David C. Mead, and William Charvat. 1965. *Prentice-Hall Handbook for Writers*. Englewood Cliffs, NJ: Prentice-Hall, Inc.

Lester, Mark, and Beason Larry. 2005. *The McGraw-Hill Handbook of English Grammar and Usage*. New York: McGraw-Hill.

Lloyd, Donald J. 1949. "The Main Drift of the English Language." *The English Journal* (The National Council of Teachers of English) 38 (8): 438-444. Accessed December 12, 2016. http://www.jstor.org/stable/807342.

McKenna, Michael. 1978. "Portmanteau Words in Reading Instruction." *Language Arts* 55 (3): 315-317. Accessed August 22, 2019. https://www.jstor.org/stable/41404624.

Merriam-Webster. 2020. *Merriam-Webster's Collegiate Dictionary*. Edited by Frederick C. Mish. Springfield, MA: Merriam-Webster, Incorporated.

—. 1994. *Merriam-Webster's Dictionary of English Usage*. Springfield, Massachusetts: Merriam-Webster, Incorporated.

Mish, Frederick C., ed. 2020. *Merriam-Webster's Collegiate Dictionary*. Eleventh. Springfield, Massachusetts: Merriam-Webster, Incorporated.

Moran, Joe. 2018. *First You Write a Sentence*. New York: Penguin Books.

N/A. n.d. *Adjectives-Word Order*. Accessed December 12, 2017. http://www.grammar.cl/rules/adjectives-word-order.gif.

O'Conner, Patricia T. 2009. *Woe Is I: The Grammarphobe's Guide to Better English in Plain English*. New York: Riverhead Books.

—. 1999. *Words Fail Me: What Everyone Who Writes Should Know About Writing.* Orlando, Florida: Harcourt, Inc.

n.d. *Perfect English Grammar: Order of Adjectives.* Accessed December 2019. www.perfect-english-grammar.com.

Pinker, Steven. 2007. *The Language Instinct: How the Mind Creates Language.* New York: HarperCollins.

—. 2011. *Words and Rules: The Ingredients of Language.* New York: Harper Perennial.

Rea, Amy. 2020. "Library Journal." *LibraryJournal.com.* April 9. Accessed November 11, 2021. https://www.libraryjournal.com/?detailStory=How-Serious-Is-Americas-Literacy-Problem.

Shaw, Harry. 1963. *Punctuate It Right.* New York: Barnes & Noble.

Stein, Sol. 1995. *Stein On Writing: A Master Editor of Some of the Most Successful Writers of Our Century Shares His Craft Techniques And Strategies.* New York: St. Martin's Griffin.

Straus, Jane. 2014. *The Blue Book of Grammar and Punctuation.* San Francisco, California: Jossey-Bass.

Strunk Jr., William, and E. B. White. 2009. *The Elements of Style.* New York: Pearson-Longman.

Thurman, Susan. 2003. *The Only Grammar Book You'll Ever Need: A One-Stop Source for Every Writing Assignment.* Avon, Massachusetts: Adams Media.

Trenga, Bonnie. 2006. *The Curious Case of the Misplaced Modifier: How to Survive the Mysteries of Weak Writing.* Cincinnati, Ohio: Writer's Digest Books.

Truss, Lynne. 2003. *Eats, Shoots & Leaves: The Zero Tolerance Approach to Punctuation.* New York: Gotham Books.

University of Chicago Press. 2017. *The Chicago Manual of Style*. Seventeenth. Chicago: University of Chicago Press.

Walsh, Bill. 2000. *Lapsing Into a Comma*. New York: McGraw-Hill.

—. 2004. *The Elephants of Style*. New York: McGraw-Hill.

Warriner, John E. 1988. *English Composition and Grammar: Complete Course*. Orlando, Florida: Harcourt Brace Jovanovich.

Wilbers, Stephen. 2000. *Keys to Great Writing*. Cincinnati, OH: Writer's Digest Books.

Withington, Robert. 1932. ""Portmanteau" Coinages." *American Speech* (Duke University Press) 7 (3): 200-203. Accessed August 22, 2019. https://www.jstor.org/stable/451651.

Withington, Robert. 1925. "Other "Portmanteau" Words." *Modern Language Notes* 40 (3): 188-189. Accessed August 22, 2019. https://www.jstor.org/stable/2914182.

Withington, Robert. 1939. "Verbal Pungencies." *American Speech* 14 (4): 269-275. Accessed August 22, 2019. https://www.jstor.org/stable/451626.

Woodward English. n.d. *Adjectives - Word Order*. Accessed December 12, 2017. http://www.grammar.cl/rules/adjectives-word-order.gif.

Zinsser, William. 2006. *On Writing Well: The Classic Guide to Writing Nonfiction*. New York: Collins.

Index

A

Academic Degree Titles, 148
acronyms, 119
active listening, 114
adjective, 17, 19, 25, 29, 72, 94, 123, 124, 161
adjective ordering, 36
Adjective Ordering, 69
Adult Literacy in the United States, 147
Advent, 167
adverb, 19, 54
advise vs. advice, 27
alot vs. a lot, 20
amazing, 74, 140
ampersand, 56
antithetical element, 36
Apostrophe Use, Misuse, and Abuse, 46
apostrophes
don't use to make words plural, 125
appositive, 34, 127
Auld Lang Syne, 174
awesome, 74, 140

B

back slash (\), 131
back-formation, 139
Bad vs. Badly, 25
baseball, 98
based *off* of, 125
based on vs. based off of, 23
Between X *to* X vs. Between X *and* X, 28
Between You and I, 49

bibliophile, 191
Bid or Bade?, 24
Bloated Writing, 75
bon appetit, 96
British English, 102
British spelling, 101
Bryan Garner, 138
bugs, 99

C

calling birds, 169
Carol, 167
Christmas, 167
Christos, 170
Classic Children's Literature video series, 146
Cliches, 93
Clippings, 103
collective nouns, 76
comma
comma splice, 40
introductory elements, 33
commas, 31, 34, 35, 36, 37, 38, 39, 40, 41, 43, 56, 101, 127
Commentate, 139
comparative form, 72
Comparison Words, 71
degree of comparison, 71
complex sentence, 62
compound sentence, 62
concerning, strange use of, 128
contraction, 17, 18, 19, 24, 127, 165
Contractions, 46
coordinate adjectives, 35
coordinating conjunction, 62
coordinating conjunctions, 33
copyediting, 176, 177

187

R

S

T

U

V

W

X

Y

Z

About the Author

Dean is a retired college educator, wearing multiple hats over a career spanning more than 22 years: academic counselor, student affairs administrator, graduate studies instructor, and research technician. Prior to that, he served in full-time Christian pastoral ministry for 16 years. He has earned master's degrees in education and ministry leadership, as well as a specialized certificate in copyediting. He has worked as a freelance copyeditor for over ten years and has written a language-related blog for more than seven years.

Dean is a bibliophile, with more books in his home library than he could read in two lifetimes, but that never stops him from acquiring more. For fun, relaxation, and professional development, he is constantly reading books and journal articles on language, grammar, usage, and writing. He also enjoys an eclectic range of fiction and nonfiction, particularly history, biography, education, current events, baseball, classic literature, and biblical studies.

He enjoys playing with his grandkids, listening to great music, strumming an acoustic guitar, eating Mexican food, cheering for the Dodgers, and savoring cinnamon rolls and clam chowder at California's Central Coast. In March 2021, Dean published a significantly revised and expanded second edition of his first book, *Nothing About Baseball Is Trivial: Essential Terms, Rules, Stats & History for Fans and Wannabe Fans.* You can find it on Amazon.

Dean and his wife reside in California's Central Valley.

NOTES

Billy: Two words are so overused nowadays that they've become practically meaningless. One of them is *awesome* and the other is *amazing*.

Bob: Wow! What *are* the two words?

NOTES

Made in the USA
Monee, IL
29 January 2022

90172293R00109